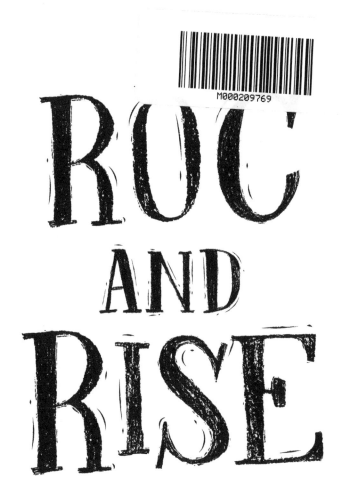

ROC AND RISE

Claire Eaton

Printed in Australia

First Edition

National Library of Australia Cataloguing-in-Publication
entry available for this title at nla.gov.au

ISBN: 978-0-6485370-0-7

Cover and Interior Design: Swish Design

To my husband Justin and son Caiden.
You're the best!

CONTENTS

INTRODUCTION 1

SECTION 1: ROC FUNDAMENTALS 23

ROC Fundamental #1: The ROC Line 26

ROC Fundamental #2: ROC Blockers and Boosters 43

ROC Fundamental #3: Heart Talk and Body Talk 46

ROC Fundamental #4: Life is STUFF 67

ROC Fundamental #5: Don't judge too harshly 86

ROC Fundamental #6: The 80:20 Rule 89

The ROC Recap - Section 1 94

SECTION 2: ROAD TO RESILIENCE 99

Name It and Claim It 105

Resilience Booster: Name it and trace it 109

Resilience Booster: The Harry Shake 110

The 6-Way Switch 114

Resilience Booster: Dream big 119

Resilience Booster: Put energy into action 125

Resilience Booster: Worry less, wish more 137

Resilience Booster: Get friendly with fear 149

Resilience Booster: Get curious 155

Resilience Booster: Soothing ROC breath 162

Resilience Booster: Catch the control freak 165

The Resilience Recap - Section 2 170

SECTION 3: BRIGHT SIDE OPTIMISM...........................175

The ROC Wish Word - Yet............................181

The ROC 5...183

Your ROC Dream Team 202

Optimism Booster: Hygge haven....................235

Optimism Booster: Music matters...................239

Optimism Booster: The power of fur friends 245

Optimism Booster: Clear clutter 249

Optimism Booster: Vision and vibe board............253

The Optimism Recap - Section 3 256

SECTION 4: CRUISING WITH CONFIDENCE 261

The Big Six 267

ROC Rituals 279

Confidence Booster: Size of the dog 289

Confidence Booster: The Love You List 292

Confidence Booster: The Learning to Love You List 293

Show Up and Shine.................................295

Where There's Shine, There's Shade 299

Make Peace With Your Shade.......................304

Time With Yourself.................................311

The Confidence Recap - Section 4 315

CONCLUSION..319

ACKNOWLEDGEMENTS.......................................329

ABOUT THE AUTHOR 331

INTRODUCTION

My teenage years were awesome. I have some of the most amazing memories, photos, experiences and stories to tell about that time of my life.

But those years were also full of surprises, blips and bumps. It was just like a rollercoaster ride really!

I had days and weeks when I was totally unstoppable, showing up with my fair share of sass and funk.

But there were also days when I was down in the dumps, following the crowd for all the wrong reasons, and looking in the mirror and judging myself way too harshly. I also spent time wondering what life was all about.

There were times when I felt rock solid in my friendships. And times I felt completely lost and out of the loop.

In sport I worked hard and was rewarded with selection for basketball teams and squads. But I also experienced the heartache and rejection of being left out of teams I desperately wanted to be in.

I remember hanging out with my friends at the beach, talking to them on the phone for hours, and laughing till my belly hurt. I have memories of going to concerts and singing my heart out as if this time in my life would never end.

But I also recall worrying about my grades, failing tests I should have passed, doubting my sporting ability, and questioning whether I should pull out of the team I'd been selected for. ("They'd have a better chance of winning without me." Right?)

I made hundreds of great decisions and choices. Looking back, they fill me with pride. But there were also monumental stuff-ups layered and scattered in between. I worked hard to fit in, and in doing so took the annoying habit of overthinking to new heights.

But with the help of my crew, family, coaches and teachers, I made it through.

After finishing high school I studied teaching at university. I went on to teach all over Western Australia in remote communities, country towns and city schools. And it was during these years that I realised the people I most loved working with were teenagers.

Teenagers like you.

And the more I read about your generation …

The more I listened to and followed you on social media …

The more I coached you in my office …

The more I presented at your schools …

The more the signs became crystal clear.

You're SO ready to step up and take full responsibility for yourself.

You want to feel more resilient, show up optimistically, and grab life's opportunities with more confidence and less worry, fear and doubt.

You want less drama in your life so you can cut to the chase and get on doing what you do best—being an awesome teenager who can be your best in this incredible game we call life.

Which brings me to this book.

Like most people my age, I muddled my way through my teenage years. As I said earlier, my life was a rollercoaster, and I rode it all the way to Year 12. If only there was a book I could have read back then to help me smooth out the ride a little.

You want to feel more resilient, show up optimistically and grab life's opportunities with more confidence, less worry, fear and doubt.

I reckon a book like that would have helped me believe in myself so much more when I was a new kid at a new school in a new country. It would have:

> » helped me learn from my dodgy choices
> » taught me why it's smart to avoid drama
> » been by my side when my high school boyfriend and I split up
> » helped me when insecurities around friendships and relationships squashed my rational thoughts
> » given me skills to hold myself up and hang on tight when:
>> » I failed tests
>> » I wasn't named in the team
>> » my mum and dad divorced
>> » I repeatedly took feedback and criticism to heart.

But there was no book. So I wrote one.

This is the book I wish I could have read when I was a teenager.

And the book you all wanted me to write. (I know this because you told me.)

You also told me you wanted more on-point skills and tools, and less statistics and doom-and-gloom stories. You're tired of playing catch-up and want to start being ahead of the game.

So let's talk about ROC.

ROC IS RESILIENCE, OPTIMISM AND CONFIDENCE DONE YOUR WAY

Why resilience, optimism and confidence? Because when I asked parents, grandparents, coaches, teachers, employers and teenagers to list their top three must-have qualities for thriving in today's world, these three were the standouts in a very long list.

Together, they let you ROC teenage life, and give you a great platform to launch into adulthood.

ROC is a way of living and learning how to keep your finger on the pulse of your thoughts, feelings, emotions and actions. It isn't fancy or complicated. It doesn't need to be. Instead it's practical, totally free and ready to use.

With ROC on your side you'll be better placed to:

» face life's ups and downs with more patience, determination, spirit and courage

» look on the bright side so you can make the most of opportunities and challenges that pop up along the way

» use your high vibe to feel good about yourself and enjoy the journey you're on

» help your friends ROC as well.

ROC IS

- ✓ Raising your resilience
- ✓ Boosting your optimism
- ✓ Lifting your confidence
- ✓ Free and portable
- ✓ Worth learning and so rewarding
- ✓ Being aware of yourself
- ✓ A way of living and loving your life
- ✓ Using boosters to help you smile on the inside
- ✓ Your right and your responsibility
- ✓ Built and mastered through daily practice of being real and authentic

ROC IS NOT

- ✗ A race to the finish line
- ✗ The same for everyone
- ✗ Always easy and without problems
- ✗ 'Set and forget' and hope for the best
- ✗ Something others can do for you
- ✗ A quick fix
- ✗ A competition to be won or lost
- ✗ Always fun and games
- ✗ Feeling happy and positive all the time
- ✗ A life without ups and downs
- ✗ Perfection

ROC invites you to discover how to become a choice maker and mindset master.

ROC REVOLVES AROUND CHOICE

Remember those Choose Your Own Adventure books? I loved them when I was younger. They'd hook me from the first chapter. And I didn't just love how the pages were filled with adventure and surprise. I also loved how, at the end of each chapter, I was invited to get involved, make decisions and choose the direction the story went.

I could turn to page 14 to board the helicopter. Or I could turn to page 17 to step aboard the boat. The choice was mine, and I loved being allowed to make that choice. I still love it.

It's powerful, and serves as a constant reminder that the foundation of a life well lived is choice.

In your life so far, you've probably made thousands of choices: some good, others wild and wacky. But don't panic if you've made a few dodgy choices along the way. You're human, and humans make mistakes.

But ROCing humans learn from them.

ROC invites you to discover how to become a **choice maker and mindset master** so you can open the gates of opportunity and put more adventure on your life agenda.

Your choices make you a mindful creator and determined ROC defender.

Are you ready to become a wise choice maker?

Would you like to become the best mindset master you can be?

Are you prepared to take charge of your own awesome adventure?

Good.

BE ROC AWARE

The first step in becoming a choice maker is to raise the bar on your own awareness. Your mission, if you choose to accept it, is to pay close attention to yourself and notice what's going on all around you.

And then you need to make this choice: will you keep reading ROC *and Rise*?

Because it's a risk.

This book is quite different to the books, podcasts and YouTube videos you're used to.

If you've got butterflies in your belly and doubtful chatter in your mind, that's okay. Those things often show up and try with all their might to stop you stepping out of your comfort zone. I won't ask you to ignore them. Instead, I'll urge you to see the butterflies and chatter as the caring kind. The kind that will allow you to answer the question, "Are you in?"

Yes?

Fantastic.

I'm so excited for you because you're standing strong at ground level and part of something really big. Your ROC adventure begins right here and right now.

ROC GIVES YOU PERMISSION TO RISE

Life will always be full of wild twists and mysterious turns. But with ROC on your side, you can show up and shine on your own terms and in your own way.

Yes, you can.

This book will prove it again and again.

And I hope you'll go on to:

» raise your RESILIENCE and look after it

» lift your OPTIMISM level and care for it

» boost your CONFIDENCE so it keeps cruising upwards.

*The first step in
becoming a choice
maker is to raise the bar
on your own awareness.*

HOW TO USE THIS BOOK

My grandad would often say to me, "Go gently my friend."

He'd whisper these wise words in my ear without any bells or whistles. He always encouraged me to keep going, and reminded me to believe in myself—one step at a time and one day at a time.

I'm whispering these words to you now. I want you to go gently too. You don't need to be a record-breaking speed reader and smash this out over the weekend, especially if that's not your style. It's not a race. Read ROC and Rise at your own speed because there are no prizes awarded for first, second or third place.

Read, stop, and talk about it.

Reflect on the ideas that pop into your head.

Ask questions, and share them with those near and dear to you.

There's no right or wrong here. But knowing you said "Yes" and have decided to read on tells me you're setting your standards high because you want to ROC and rise.

You should read the book from start to finish. Each section builds on the one before, and sets the scene for the next. Then go back to revise and re-read, or simply open the page that's calling your name.

Read the stories and complete the ROC rituals and boosters. If you use them consistently you'll have a better chance of:

» putting yourself out there

» taking smart risks

» accepting challenges

» recovering when you make mistakes.

Which is how you're going to ROC and rise.

GET READY FOR REMINDERS

You might come across some information you've heard before. You know it, but you skipped over it because it was too hard, or you didn't understand it at the time. That's okay. Here's another chance to be totally accountable to yourself: read the chapters and do the work.

Why? Because you're worth it.

BE PREPARED TO BE CHALLENGED

Some words, questions and ideas will grab your attention and prompt you to find out more about yourself. Don't be surprised if you find yourself wanting to research a topic more to fill your curious mind. You may even start up conversations you've avoided in the past. It's what

ROCers do. Let your confidence build, dive in, explore, and follow your own ROC path.

BUT PLEASE BE WARNED

If you read this book, do the boosters, rituals, switches, and spend time thinking about the Big Six, you'll probably start noticing changes within yourself. You'll be getting to know yourself on a whole new level. You'll feel so damn empowered that nothing will stand in your way. And if anything tried to, you'll have the ROC power to handle it.

OWN THIS BOOK!

Keep it with you and make it your own. Welcome it into your mind, your heart and your home. Write all over it, dog ear the corners, highlight the parts that pop for you, and don't let it out of your sight. It will become your precious 'go to' book. It's filled with ROC gold. Treasure it, and guard it with your life.

Keep it on the kitchen bench, on the coffee table, beside your bed, and within reach of the bathtub. Take it with you on holiday and long road trips. If it's with you, you're more likely to open it and read what you need.

Make it a part of your daily life. Discuss it with your friends, flick through pages together, and crack open the bits and pieces that inspire you the most.

If you read this book,
there is a very strong
chance that you will
notice changes within
yourself.

Turn the pages with an open mind, because everything you read will serve you well today, tomorrow and throughout your amazing life.

Go gently my friend. That's my hope for you, as it was my grandad's hope for me.

This book is divided into four sections:

PART 1: ROC FUNDAMENTALS

It's all about ROC: what it means, why you want it, and how to get it. Don't skip this—you'll regret it if you do.

PART 2: ROAD TO RESILIENCE

This is the engine room of ROC. It has classic stories, boosters and mindset switches that will teach you ways to think and feel ROC. Each section will give you a new skill you can use to bounce back, dust yourself off and feel stronger whenever life puts problems, complications or tricky times in your way.

PART 3: BRIGHT SIDE OPTIMISM

Who doesn't love being around an optimist? They are the bright-side thinkers who live life with a glass that's half full of ROC goodness. This part of the book shares 16 of my favourite optimism boosting tools. Get ready to reveal your inner optimist so you can rise in ways you may never have thought possible.

PART 4: CRUISING WITH CONFIDENCE

Confidence comes in all shapes and sizes, and looks completely different on everyone. This part of the book is gold because it's the how-to guide to boosting your confidence from the inside out. There are 14 simple-to-use confidence boosters ready to put to good use at home, events, sport, parties with your friends, and in situations where you need confidence on your side.

Together these sections will expose you to more than 50 ways to ROC and rise!

It's time to raise the bar, crush your inner critic, and let your ROC roar louder than you ever thought possible.

Let's do this thing!

ONE PAGE

ONE IDEA

ONE STORY

ONE BOOSTER

ONE TACTIC

ONE SWITCH

ONE REMINDER

ONE **DAY AT A TIME**

Notes & ROC Reminders

Take some time to reflect on what you've read in the Introduction. What caught your eye? What thoughts and ideas were triggered? What do you want to make sure you don't forget?

_____

_____

_____

_____

_____

_____

_____

_____

_____

_____

_____

_____

SECTION 1
ROC FUNDAMENTALS

ROC FUNDAMENTALS

Who doesn't love a road trip? You're up early, the sun is shining, and excitement fills the air as bags and boxes flow out of the house and into the car. But before you hit the road you need to take care of a few fundamentals—no ifs, buts or excuses—that will set you up for a smooth ride.

Road trip fundamentals:

1. Tyres – good to go.
2. Windscreen wiper water – topped up.
3. Petrol tank – filled.
4. Headlights – checked.
5. House locked and secure – done.
6. Plenty of water and delicious snacks packed – yes and yes.

You can't skip these road trip fundamentals. You need to tick them off one by one before you start your journey.

Your ROC journey also has six fundamentals:

1. The ROC line
2. ROC blockers and boosters
3. Heart talk and body talk
4. Life is STUFF
5. Don't judge too harshly
6. The 80:20 rule

Taking the time to learn, practise and master these fundamentals will give you the best chance to have an awesome ROC journey.

Let's do it.

ROC FUNDAMENTAL #1: THE ROC LINE

First up, let me introduce you to the ROC line.

Take a moment to lift your eyes and gaze at the lay of the land. Whether you're looking at a paddock of wheat or waves on the beach you'll see the horizon—a natural line separating earth from the sky and the stars above.

Nature's line will help you imagine the ROC line, which divides the ups and downs within you.

The line separates your **thoughts, feelings, emotions and behaviours** into two sections.

The top section is 'above-the-line', and the lower section is 'below-the-line'.

ABOVE-THE-LINE

BELOW-THE-LINE

This ROC line is the foundation for each ROC tool you'll read about in this book. And I hope it becomes a regular part of your mental fitness vocabulary.

The line is completely mobile, and is with you 24/7. As a beginner you may want to draw it on a piece of paper to get the hang of it. But eventually you'll be able to draw it in your mind, which makes it even more mobile.

The line serves as a visual cue as you ask yourself, "Am I below or above the line right now?"

Humans naturally play on both sides of the horizon. We walk on land and fly in the sky. And neither is good or bad, better or worse. It's just what it is. Sometimes you're up and sometimes you're down.

Neither is good or bad, better or worse. It's just what it is. Sometimes you're up and sometimes you're down.

It's normal.

It's okay.

It's to be expected.

It's impossible not to be that way. (Unless you're a robot that's been programmed to live a perfect life in a perfect world.)

Both sides of the ROC line have an incredibly important role to play in your ROC journey. But here's something you need to know right off the bat: throughout your life you will experience both sides of the line—over and over again. Yes, you will. That's life.

Neither side of the line can exist without the other.

Right now you could be dancing above the line or diving below it. That's okay. You might flutter up and down next week too. The game of life will never stop surprising you. But how you play that game is totally up to you.

Getting to know this ROC line is probably the most important step you can take on your ROC *and Rise* adventure.

To ROC you must **tune into you**.

To RISE you must **act on everything you tune into**.

Let's start by diving below the line.

BELOW-THE-LINE

Here are some examples of **below-the-line** words and phrases written by teenagers just like you. Of course, this collection is just a drop in the ocean because there are hundreds of below-the-line words that could be included.

worried angry lonely frustrated rude

pressured disrespectful SAD

short tempered gossiping anxious

cynical disappointed stubborn helpless

ashamed upset hopeless grumpy ignoring

resentment regretful guilty judging

scared crying isolating insecure fake

unmotivated shame NEGATIVE uptight

pessimistic holding a grudge

closed-minded fearful stuck bullying

annoyed overwhelmed frowning lying

fighting putdowns stupid stressed

ROC TASK: REFLECTING LOW

Now that you've read all those below-the-line words, try to write down what you're thinking. How do you feel? What do you see in your mind? Can you hear a particular sound or wise word being spoken?

_____

_____

_____

_____

_____

Are there any below-the-line words you would add to the collection?

_____

_____

_____

_____

_____

*To ROC you must tune
into you. To RISE you
must act on everything
you tune into.*

ABOVE-THE-LINE

Now let's flip it. Here are some examples of **above-the-line** words and phrases. I'm sure you can add a million more.

*kind peaceful hopeful motivated
sincere accepting courageous relaxed
POSITIVE loyal compassionate brave
open–minded truthful reliable healthy
caring sympathetic authentic laughing
humour optimistic determined gracious
responsible smiling welcoming giving
empathetic fairness excited
at ease resilient grateful encouraging
proud complimentary believing
respectful helpful trusting calm honest
friendly forgiving loving being yourself
enthusiastic HAPPY confident*

ROC TASK: REFLECTING HIGH

After reading these words, try to write down what you're thinking now. How do you feel? What can you see in your mind? Can you hear a sound or a wise voice?

_____

_____

_____

_____

_____

_____

What words would you add to the list?

_____

_____

_____

_____

_____

_____

You probably noticed a massive difference in the energy and vibe between each group of words. Powerful, isn't it?

So why do I call this ROC tool "above- and below-the-line"? Why didn't I call it "positive and negative", "happy and sad", or even "good thinking and bad thinking"?

Because being human is so much more than being happy or sad, positive or negative, or even feeling good or bad. Life just isn't that clear cut.

Life is a big, magical mix of above- and below-the-line thoughts, feelings, emotions and behaviours. They all work in weird and wonderful ways, depending on what's going on in your life.

Diving in.

'Sad' and 'negative' are only two of the words in our below-the-line collection. Life is a whirlpool of heavier, slower and harder thoughts, feelings and emotions. So it's crazy to make these two words carry the burden when you're feeling flat, lonely or just out of sorts. It's time to change that so you can expand your below-the-line vocabulary and accurately explain what's going on in your mind, heart and body.

*ROC is learning how
to show up and play in
both arenas—
below the line and
above the line.*

Flipping it.

'Happy' and 'positive' are only two of the words in our above-the-line collection. But they're often overused, putting a lot of unfair pressure on you to be happy and to be positive *all the time*. The collection of thoughts, feelings and emotions proves there's more to life as a human being than being happy and positive.

ROC is learning how to show up and play in both arenas—below the line *and* above the line.

You'll go up and you'll go down. But by reading this book I hope you choose to use all the ROC boosters ahead to help you get up and stay above the line as much as you can.

However, you need to be realistic. Keep in mind that you're human with a heartbeat. And just as your heart rate will rise and fall depending on the situation, so too will your ROC heart.

Imaginary lines divide people,
land, countries and states.
Lines in your mind make your life
one big ROC adventure.
It's your time to choose and create.

ABOVE-THE-LINE

*kind peaceful hopeful motivated accepting helpful
courage relaxed positive authentic loyal compassion
brave open-minded truthful authentic friendly
laughing humour determined gracious responsibility
optimistic smiling welcoming giving empathy fairness
excited at ease resilient grateful encouraging proud
complimenting believing respectful trusting
calm honest forgiving trust love being yourself
enthusiastic happy confident*

IT'S YOUR CHOICE

*worried angry lonely frustrated rude pressured
disrespectful sad short tempered gossiping anxious
cynical disappointed stubborn helpless ashamed upset
hopeless stressed grumpy ignoring resentment regretful
guilty judging scared crying isolating insecure fake
unmotivated shame negative uptight pessimistic
holding a grudge closed-minded fearful stuck bullying
annoyed overwhelmed frowning lying fighting
putdowns stupid excluding mean*

BELOW-THE-LINE

THE NATURAL ROCER

Have you ever believed that some people were born with a bucketload of ROC? They seem to glide through life, catch the curve balls, bounce back with ease, and enter a room without missing a beat. There's something about those people that's hard to put into words. They look ROC solid.

I call these people Natural ROCers. The world is filled with natural artists, athletes and scientists who were born to paint, run and solve the most complex mysteries. So it makes sense that some people are born into the world to ROC. (Lucky ducks.)

If you meet a Natural ROCer, or there's a Natural ROCer in your friendship group, resist the temptation to get sucked into the crazy comparison trap. It's a first-class ROC blocker, and a great way to stop yourself from rising.

If you are a Natural ROCer, congratulations. Be proud, and keep on believing, building and backing yourself. It can be easy to hold yourself back and not shine as you should.

Have you heard of Tall Poppy Syndrome?

Imagine looking at a field of hundreds of stunning red poppies. One poppy catches your eye. It's doing what it was grown to do, but it's taller, more upright, and a little brighter than the other poppies in the field.

Imagine that standout poppy being singled out and cut down just because it's rising and shining as it should. That's so unfair.

Imagine that standout poppy being singled out and cut down just because it's rising and shining as it should. That's so unfair.

When you're a Natural ROCer you stand tall, strong and bright like that tall poppy in the field. But sometimes your Natural ROCer status isn't celebrated. Instead you're seen as a threat or competition, and you're at risk of being cut down. So you try not to stand so tall, and sadly you blend in with the crowd. It can even be your friends and teammates who use putdowns, sarcasm, social media and exclusion to chop you back down to size.

Tall Poppy Syndrome can cause ROCers to stay small. You don't stand out in the crowd. Instead you dim your light to fit in. That's a crying shame, because not only do you miss out on shining as you should, but the world misses out on your sunshine. If you've been blocked from rising once, I hope this book gives you the boosters you need to have another go and rise again.

Would you like to ROC more?

Would you like to help your friends ROC and rise?

If you answered "Yes" then you're reading the right book.

Be proud.
Be humble.
Believe in yourself.
Back yourself.

There's a place in the field for everyone:
The natural ROCer
The rookie ROCer
The reluctant ROCer
The champion ROCer.

Be a tall poppy.
ROC and rise.
As you should.

ROC FUNDAMENTAL #2: ROC BLOCKERS AND BOOSTERS

ROC BLOCKERS

ROC blockers lurk around stealthily, and try to fool you into believing you're not good enough, smart enough, fast enough, kind enough, tall enough or happy enough.

They can be quite brutal.

You don't often see them. Instead you hear them in your mind when your thoughts plummet below the line, and feel them in your heart and body.

So what is a ROC blocker? Here are the top five blockers written by people your age.

1. Putting yourself second, third, fourth or fifth, and listening too much to the thoughts and opinions of strangers or friends. This is dangerous and layered in extreme risk.
   Avoid, avoid, avoid.

2. Comparing yourself to others in unkind ways ("She's more popular", "He's more talented") is exhausting, and pushes you down a slippery slide to below the line.
   The comparison trap is a dangerous place to be. It leaves you feeling empty and uninspired.

*Avoiding challenges
or being involved
in anything new or
different freezes your
freedom and robs you of
your natural spark.*

3. Focussing on everything you can't do, aren't very good at, or have done wrong in the past.
   It clouds your vision and hides your unique talent, beauty and grit, making them hard to see.

4. Avoiding challenges or being involved in anything new or different to what you usually do, just in case you fail, look silly, stuff up or get bored.
   It freezes your freedom and robs you of your natural spark.

5. Concentrating on, reading about and speaking about all the bad things, sad news, 'doom and gloom' stories, tales of disaster and negativity in the world.
   It brings you down. Go there at your own peril.

Blockers hold you back from being your most resilient, optimistic and confident self.

ROC BOOSTERS

This book is filled with ROC boosters—practical tools, tips and tactics ready for you to learn, choose and use when you:

> » fall below the line and want to climb back up above the line
>
> » are above the line and want to stay there and enjoy the view.

As you read this book, you'll become quicker at noticing when you're blocking yourself from ROCing. And yes, most of time you are the biggest blocker in your life.

But with practice you'll become more aware of it, and form the habit of boosting instead of blocking yourself. And each time you do it you'll raise your own resilience, optimism and confidence from the inside out.

Nice.

ROC FUNDAMENTAL #3: HEART TALK AND BODY TALK

At the epicentre of ROC are your thoughts, which you read about in ROC Fundamental #1. Your below- or above-the-line thoughts create a naturally occurring ripple effect that breathes life to your emotions and feelings (heart talk).

I was reminded of this when I began coaching 15-year-old Zac in Year 10. He was trying to make sense of his below-the-line thoughts that were increasing and making him feel out of sorts.

When Zac and I met he explained he had become an expert at ignoring his emotions and feelings. He felt weak and embarrassed when his emotions fell below the line. He went on to explain that to feel better he pushed them away, squashing them into an imaginary box in his mind. He hoped they wouldn't return and wreak havoc in his mind.

But in this case, hope wasn't enough. Heart talk always finds its way.

'Heart talk' is a phrase I use to describe all feelings and emotions, whether they're below- or above-the-line. Heart talk and its close friend 'body talk' (body feelings and sensations) are both signalling systems that can help you regulate and manage your ROC level.

Acknowledging your below-the-line heart talk is such a brave, clever and strong above-the-line habit to practice.

If you think it's embarrassing or weak to have below-the-line heart talk, keep reading. I want to prove you wrong.

Acknowledging your below-the-line heart talk is such a brave, clever and strong above-the-line habit to practise. And it will boost your ROC level more than you can imagine.

Emotions and feelings, especially those below-the-line, can be incredibly strong. But I believe they have a purpose, and show up for a reason. They remind you what's important to you and what is not. They teach you lessons in life and pave the way to increased self-awareness, so you can continue getting to know yourself from the inside out.

HEART TALK

No one is exempt from heart talk. Experiencing it on both sides of the ROC line is completely normal and to be expected. This was clear to see when I asked more than 300 high school students to list the ways that their heart talks below and above the ROC line.

Here's what they wrote.

TOP 10 HEART TALK — BELOW-THE-LINE EMOTIONS AND FEELINGS

- » 1   *Doubt*
- » 2   *Anger*
- » 3   *Worry*
- » 4   *Fear*
- » 5   *Failure*

- » 6   *Stress*
- » 7   *Overwhelm*
- » 8   *Disappointment*
- » 9   *Loneliness*
- » 10   *Jealousy*

TOP 10 HEART TALK — ABOVE-THE-LINE EMOTIONS AND FEELINGS

- » 1   *Love*
- » 2   *Pride*
- » 3   *Surprise*
- » 4   *Confidence*
- » 5   *Happiness*

- » 6   *Motivated*
- » 7   *Relaxed*
- » 8   *Positive*
- » 9   *Safe*
- » 10   *Calm*

ROC TASK: OBSERVE YOUR HEART TALK

Over the next few days, tune into your emotions and feelings.

Write the words that best describe your below-the-line heart talk—the words that match the chitter chatter in your heart. Don't judge or overthink. Just write. There are no right or wrong answers.

_____

_____

_____

_____

Write all the words that match your above-the-line heart talk here. Remember, this space will probably feel lighter and brighter because it's the bright side of life.

_____

_____

_____

_____

_____

*Their body talk
suggested their thoughts
were above the line and
flying high.*

BODY TALK

Body talk was loud and clear on a classic day in September 2018.

When the final siren echoed around the Melbourne Cricket Ground (MCG), the capacity crowd witnessed an epic moment in football history.

The West Coast Eagles had just beaten Collingwood by five points. The difference between celebration and devastation was less than a goal.

Twenty-two men suddenly grew taller and so much bigger as they threw their arms high in the air. Of course they did. They were the winners. They ran and soared, cheered and roared, because together they had won the AFL Grand Final—the ultimate football honour.

And while we'll never know for sure, their body talk suggested their thoughts were above the line and flying high:

» Winner!

» We deserve this

» I played my part

» I'm so proud

» Our hard work paid off for us

» We won!

In stark contrast were the losers—22 men who had suddenly become small and static. They lay on the ground where their sporting hopes had just been crushed in four short quarters. Heads down, eyes closed and shoulders slumped, they covered their faces with their hands to protect their stolen dreams and shattered hearts.

If anyone was watching the television with the sound off, they would know without a shadow of a doubt who had won and who had lost. The bodies of 44 men and their support crew held no secrets. Their body talk said it all.

Winners in yellow and blue, rising and expanding.

Losers in black and white, falling and shrinking.

This moment served as a brazen reminder that your thoughts (psychology) trigger your heart talk and body talk (physiology), which then prompt you to behave the way you do. In this case, the Eagles went wild, bathing in well-deserved winners' euphoria.

Your body talk is a vital part of your ROCability. It serves as an early warning system. If you notice your heart talk and body talk, you will be led back to the core of it all—your thoughts.

Higher, brighter and lighter thoughts will help your body appear more open, taller, relaxed, at ease, certain and confident. That's what the winners were doing, as were their passionate supporters.

On the flipside, under the weight of lower, slower and heavier thinking your body will more likely shrink and slouch, with your head down and your arms low. That's what the losers were doing, along with their dedicated supporters.

By paying close attention to your heart talk and body talk, you'll become more aware of your thoughts. And this knowledge will give you the power to choose your own adventure every day of your life.

If your eyes are the window to your soul,
your heart talk and body talk are the doorways
to your wild and wondering thoughts.

Noticing other people's body talk is always easier than noticing your own. It takes bravery to intentionally observe yourself. But as you've probably already noticed, it's a big part of ROCing and rising.

When you face a
problem or unexpected
challenge, your body
talk might scare you,
or even leave you
wondering if you've
lost control.

To ROC, you must be aware of yourself.
To RISE, you must act on what
you've become aware of.

I've never met anyone who doesn't want to be above the line at school, in sport, with friends, at home, or at work on their weekend shift. There's usually a lot more joy, laughter, calm and peace up there. And that means there's probably less worry, doubt, fear, stress and overwhelm cluttering up your mind, your day and your life.

When you face a problem or an unexpected challenge, your body can feel like it's reacting in crazy ways. Your body talk might scare you, or even leave you wondering if you've lost control. The flood gates open, and panic and anxiety quickly rush in. Really quickly. It feels revolting, uncomfortable and hard to shake off.

Cortisol and adrenaline (the body's stress response chemicals) are released, triggering a glucose hit that makes your body fire up and defend you in the most mind-boggling ways. (It's like the sugar hit you get after eating a lot of chocolate. As you eat, your body reacts, and you quickly hit a high. Unfortunately, you quickly plummet to a thundering low soon after. Chocolate lovers, we feel your pain.)

What's annoying is these natural stress chemicals can stay in your system for quite a while, making you feel unsettled, stressed and anxious long after you asked the questions and didn't know the answers.

You can imagine what will happen if you repeat this pattern for a few days, or even weeks. Your body will be in a constant state of alertness, which can trap you in a world of worried, fearful, doubtful and anxious thinking.

Yuck.

You know the feeling of panic, and how it can consume you when your thoughts spiral down below the line? Let's shine some light on that so you've got some handy tools to use when you're gripped by anxiety and panic.

In these situations, intentional breathing is a great way to help soothe your nervous system. (You can find out more about ROC breathing on page 162.)

But let's hit this revolting feeling head on, look it in the eyes, and strip it of its power.

Anxiousness is a normal human emotion. But I'm sure you'll agree it's one huge below-the-line pain in the butt that needs to back off when you tell it to. When anxiousness shows up, you need some serious ROC tools to sort it out and put it back in its place.

Let's be honest: when your body talk gets so out of control it feels like you're being attacked by something, somehow or somewhere, your self-belief takes a hit and you start to hide away.

Your body talk can be so powerful that it stops you from being yourself—meeting new people, going to the beach, contributing to group chats, even going to parties with friends.

Sound familiar?

Your tummy flips, your mouth is dry, and your heart feels like it's beating out of your chest. You become trapped in a holding pattern of below-the-line thinking, which only makes the body talk worse. Each fuels the other and the pattern continues.

It's a horrible feeling. In fact, 'horrible' probably isn't a strong enough word to describe it. You probably have your own word to describe this hideous and revolting feeling that needs to take a hike.

In those moments when it feels like your body has gone on a crazy ride to another planet, I want you to do one thing: **observe your own body talk.**

But first, I'd like to explain why your body behaves in such a weird, wild and wacky fashion, as if you're out of control and have lost your way.

*When anxiousness
shows up, you need
some serious ROC tools
to sort it out and put it
back in its place.*

Working with young people and teaching ROC mindset tools, I've found it's the teenagers who work hard to become experts in observing their body talk that find it easiest to recover and climb back up above the line.

Your BODY TALK
is a reliable part of your
ROC management system.
It reflects the
THOUGHTS in your mind and
EMOTIONS in your heart.

No one escapes body talk. I asked more than 300 students to write a list of all the ways their body might talk to indicate they've fallen below the line. They did the same for above-the-line body talk too.

I asked them not to judge, compare or compete, but just write how their body talks, and then drop it in the boxes left on the stage.

Here's what they wrote.

TOP 15 BODY TALK BELOW-THE-LINE WORDS

» 1 *Sore or sick stomach feeling*

» 2 *Crying, teary, trembling chin*

» 3 *Hot or cold body temperature*

» 4 *Sweaty hands*

» 5 *Heart beats faster*

» 6 *Dry mouth, hard to swallow*

» 7 *Can't get your words out*

» 8 *Slumped shoulders and head down*

» 9 *Red face and neck*

» 10 *Headaches and migraines*

» 11 *Shaking hands and wobbly legs*

» 12 *Flat tone of voice*

» 13 *Gasping or holding breath*

» 14 *Clenched teeth and jaw*

» 15 *Tense and fidgety body*

TOP 15 BODY TALK ABOVE-THE-LINE WORDS

» 1   *Relaxed stomach*

» 2   *Smiling*

» 3   *Laughing*

» 4   *Regular body temperature*

» 5   *Steady or excited heartbeat*

» 6   *Friendly facial expressions*

» 7   *Fluent speech and tone of voice*

» 8   *Open posture and head up*

» 9   *Normal skin tone*

» 10   *Eyes gentle and focused*

» 11   *Sturdy and stable body*

» 12   *Soft hands*

» 13   *Regular breathing*

» 14   *Relaxed teeth and jaw*

» 15   *Being yourself body gestures*

*Your body talk can
be so powerful that it
stops you from being
yourself.*

ROC TASK: OBSERVE YOUR BODY TALK

Over the next few days, tune into your emotions.

Write the words that best describe your below-the-line body talk.

_____

_____

_____

_____

_____

Write your above-the-line body talk words here. Remember, they're more likely to feel lighter and brighter.

_____

_____

_____

_____

_____

HEART TALK AND BODY TALK IN ACTION

As you can see, your thoughts have consequences. They trigger your heart talk and your body talk, which in turn trigger your actions and behaviours.

Here are two examples, one heading below the line and the other above it.

EXAMPLE 1

Thought – I'll be on my own at the party and I won't know who to talk to or what to do.

Heart Talk – Scared, nervous, anxious, worried.

Body Talk – Sick tummy, tight shoulders, crazy wild butterflies.

Behaviour – Find a way to avoid going at all. Create an excuse or even repeat your thoughts, heart talk and body talk so often that you feel too unwell to even think about going to the party.

Result – Didn't go to the party and lost an opportunity to practice being resilient.

EXAMPLE 2

Thought – I'll be on my own at the party. But hopefully I'll be introduced to people and get to know them. I can't wait to see my friend on her birthday and meet her other friends too. It's great to be included and invited.

Heart Talk – A little scared, nervous and anxious, but also really excited, curious and happy.

Body Talk – A little funny in the tummy, shoulders a bit tight, and a few butterflies. But you're smiling, with your head up and your eyes are starting to sparkle.

Behaviour – Arrange a time to be dropped off and ask your friend to meet you when you arrive.

Result – Go to the party and make the most of the opportunity to practise being resilient.

ROC FUNDAMENTAL #4: LIFE IS STUFF

STUFF is the ROC word that covers everything and anything that shows up in your life. STUFF is neither good nor bad, positive or negative, until you decide how you're going to think about it. (You'll learn more about it in the next fundamental.)

*No matter how
old you are, you'll
always have STUFF
in your life.*

Here's a general STUFF list, shared by ROC students just like you.

- ✓ homework
- ✓ appearance
- ✓ health
- ✓ pets
- ✓ food
- ✓ sleep
- ✓ devices
- ✓ games
- ✓ teachers
- ✓ tests
- ✓ sport
- ✓ injuries
- ✓ friendships
- ✓ money
- ✓ part-time job
- ✓ team selection
- ✓ glasses
- ✓ school uniform
- ✓ rules
- ✓ hearing aid

- ✓ music
- ✓ parties
- ✓ clothes
- ✓ shoes
- ✓ weather
- ✓ technology
- ✓ social media
- ✓ magazines
- ✓ emails
- ✓ fashion
- ✓ puberty
- ✓ fast food
- ✓ traffic
- ✓ team mates
- ✓ winning
- ✓ sexuality
- ✓ holidays
- ✓ world news
- ✓ exercise

- ✓ driving
- ✓ parents
- ✓ siblings
- ✓ recess
- ✓ airport
- ✓ books
- ✓ opinions
- ✓ alcohol
- ✓ curfews
- ✓ birthdays
- ✓ animals
- ✓ gifts
- ✓ rain
- ✓ festivals
- ✓ beach
- ✓ summer
- ✓ seeding and harvest
- ✓ neighbours
- ✓ braces

No matter how old you are, you'll always have STUFF in your life. It will probably change depending on your age and the stage you're at in your life.

STUFF can be temporary or permanent. But whatever category it falls into, you have all you need inside you to make the best of it, handle it, or ride it out. We can't immunise ourselves against failure, bad news, tragedy, heartbreak or misadventure. Humans don't have that much power.

You may have noticed that STUFF shifts to a whole new level as life hurls events, situations and experiences your way that nothing in your wildest dreams can prepare you for. Very few humans live their life without experiencing something that hurts so bad they wonder if they'll ever be able to get back above the line.

Everyone has their own personal extreme STUFF to deal with, so I can't give you a detailed list. Everyone's journey is so different. For me, losing my dog Sonni was gut wrenching, and saying goodbye to my adored grandparents was heartbreaking. I really struggled in my final year of high school. And I clearly remember the intense homesickness I felt when I was 20 and teaching in Oombulgurri, a remote Aboriginal community more than 3,000kms from my home in Perth.

Some STUFF speaks its own universal language that's immersed in unspeakable heartache, confusion, grief and loss. This calls for another level of self-care, kindness and time to heal because you can't outrun feelings and emotions no matter how hard you try. You're a precious human, and you need time to do whatever feels right for you when your heart is broken and you're trying to relight your beautiful candle.

Think back to Year Four when your classroom seating setup was the biggest thing on your mind. It was on the top of your STUFF list. Now that you're older, your list is probably more complex and may include your part-time job, tests, fashion, friendships, and events on your social calendar.

Life is jam-packed with STUFF.

Life is full of STUFF.
STUFF is life.
YOUR LIFE. YOUR STUFF.
No-one is EXEMPT.

It's time to have at closer look at your STUFF list.

WARNING:

When talking about STUFF, don't fall into the comparison trap.

Their life, their STUFF.

Your life, your STUFF.

Sharing and talking is awesome.

Comparing and judging is not.

Write down all the STUFF in your life. If it jumps into your mind, put it in the box. Remember, there's no good or bad, positive or negative. You're just naming the things on your mind and in your life right now.

My STUFF List

Your STUFF list is personal.

Whether you talk about it with friends is up to you. It can be a great thing to do, and you might even discover you have some STUFF in common.

In a good old-fashioned face-to-face STUFF chat, you'll probably learn more about your friend than you thought you knew. Your friendship could even soar to a higher level.

ROC BOOSTER: CHANCE TO CHOOSE

High school students instantly jump on board when they realise they can choose how they think about STUFF in their life. We create a 'STUFF list' on a massive whiteboard. It usually has about 30 words, but it could potentially have hundreds or even thousands of words because STUFF is endless—from birds and bikes to rain and reality TV shows. That's what keeps life interesting.

To demonstrate the power of choice I invite students to select a word from the list. And the words they usually choose are 'homework', 'tests' or 'exams'.

Notice the automatic thought response you had to the word 'homework'? Chances are it was "I like it", "I don't like it", or something far, far worse. That thought may be true and accurate for you, and that's fine.

You're human, and so you'll have STUFF in your life that doesn't float your boat. I'm not a raving fan of dentist appointments. To be honest, I don't just loathe them, I'm quite fearful of them too. But rather than being fake and saying I like going to the dentist, I tell it like it is. There's no space for fake here. I haven't got the energy for that.

I choose thoughts that will help me get to the dentist every year. Why? Because I want to look after my teeth, prevent problems occurring in the future, and avoid big dental bills whenever I can.

You're allowed to dislike some music, events, places, chores and people that pop into your life. But you also have all the ROC boosters you need to choose how you think, feel and behave.

Here's the game changer.

Thinking below-the-line or above-the-line is your choice. But as you've just learned, your thoughts have a profound ripple effect on your heart talk and body talk. And this ripple effect can flow all the way through to your behaviour.

Let's see how you can build your mental fitness by applying the Chance to Choose ROC booster to 'homework'.

First, we acknowledge the basic facts about the word.

Homework is STUFF. It's an eight-letter compound noun. That's its claim to fame.

Beyond the facts, you'll make up the rest of the story. You'll flick back through memories of when you forgot your homework, lost it, or felt confused and totally stuck while doing it. Your thoughts may leap above the line as you recall completing tasks, getting great scores,

Being fake is pointless and energy draining. Why fill your mind with thoughts that are untrue?

and success along the way. You might even remember how homework affected your home and family. Did it bring you closer together or drive you further apart?

If you dislike homework as much as I dislike dentist appointments, that's okay. But here's the thing, ongoing and repetitive thoughts of dislike can block you from moving forward.

Being fake is pointless and energy draining. Why fill your mind with thoughts that are untrue (at least for you)? Trying to catapult your thinking back above the line with the opposite thought ("I love homework" or "I love the dentist") is riddled with danger.

If it's not true, you don't believe it and you don't feel comfortable saying it, then don't say it.

Fake is hard work. Really hard.
There's a better way.

Be real and accept your own opinions. Then you can decide how you'll approach the STUFF you're not keen on. Homework is STUFF (whether you like it, love it or loathe it).

Here are some of the most common above- and below-the-line thoughts about homework.

I'll feel good when it's all done

I need to learn this information

It will help me prepare for my test

I'll be able to hand it in on time

It's a part of school, so I need to get on with it

I'll plan it out so it's more doable

I can ask for help if I need it

─────────── **YOUR CHOICE** ───────────

It's such a waste of time

I can't be bothered so I won't do it

I've done enough at school already

I've got better things to do with my time

I'm not interested in this

I'll make excuses

It's too hard

BELOW-THE-LINE THINKING CAN LEAD YOU AWAY FROM HOMEWORK COMPLETION.

Add your own below-the-line thoughts here:

_____

_____

_____

Ripple effect: Reflecting on your thoughts, how does your heart talk and body talk?

_____

_____

_____

Ripple effect: With awareness of your thoughts, heart talk and body talk, how might you behave? What choices would you make? What actions would you take?

_____

_____

_____

_____

_____

Be real and accept your own opinions. Then you can decide how you'll approach the STUFF you're not keen on.

ABOVE-THE-LINE THINKING GIVES YOU A BETTER CHANCE OF GETTING YOUR HOMEWORK DONE.

Add your thoughts here:

_____

_____

_____

Ripple effect: Given your thoughts, how do your heart and body talk?

_____

_____

_____

Ripple effect: With awareness of your thoughts, heart talk and body talk, how might you behave now? What choices would you make? What actions would you take?

_____

_____

_____

_____

_____

Choose your vibe.

Think on the bright side.

Here's your chance to try this booster on an item from your STUFF list.

FIVE BOOSTING STEPS

1. Go back to your STUFF list on page 73. Choose an item you know you have an automatic below-the-line thought response towards.

_____

_____

_____

_____

_____

2. Jot down a few of your below-the-line thoughts.

_____

_____

_____

_____

3. Write a few above-the-line thoughts you could think instead. (This may take more time because you're so used to thinking about it in a below-the-line way. Stick with it.)

_____

_____

_____

_____

4. Circle your top two above-the-line thoughts.

_____

_____

_____

5. Say those top two above-the-line thoughts out loud, noticing how your heart talk and body talk shifts to match your thoughts.

_____

_____

_____

_____

*Your new thoughts will
prompt you to react and
respond in a way that lifts
you above the line.*

Remember your original dislike for the STUFF? It may not have changed, and that's okay. But your new thoughts will prompt you to react and respond in a way that lifts you above the line. And believe me, it's much nicer up there.

You need only brave the wilderness.
Let your thoughts lead you into nature's space
where colour, sound, peace and

W

O

N

D

E

R

awaits.

ROC FUNDAMENTAL #5: DON'T JUDGE TOO HARSHLY

As an eight-year-old girl I'd balance on a rickety wooden stool, leaning over a deep-water sink filled with dirty dishes and white fluffy foam.

Beside me was a grand man I called Grandad, sporting an impressive grey beard and holding a thick cotton tea towel.

In his younger days, Grandad was a WWII paratrooper in the British Elite Forces. He jumped out of planes and landed in war-torn Africa, Italy, Greece, France and Germany. He trusted his life to his parachute—a thin layer of Japanese silk that he alone was responsible for folding and precisely packing before every single jump. They didn't have backup chutes in those days, and so accuracy and attention to detail couldn't be overlooked. Knowing this, it made so much sense that he was such a stickler for doing things right and doing them well. Every time he jumped from an aeroplane, his life depended on it.

In the kitchen, the silk parachute was replaced with a blue and white striped cotton tea towel and Grandad was ready to dry the dishes and put them away. As he lifted each dish he'd pause for a moment to build suspense, and with his scrutinous eye look for the reject—the plate that wasn't clean and didn't meet strict standards.

It was inevitable that he would find the reject, because as you know, not everything in life is perfect.

When he found it he'd stand to attention like a sergeant addressing his troops. With his eyebrows raised and a cheeky smile on his face, he would announce in his loudest military voice that he did indeed have a reject in his hand.

And without hesitation he would return the reject to the dirty dishes pile.

Winking at me in true grandad style, he'd say that dishes need to be clean and of course I was up for the job. We had proof. He'd point to all the sparkling glasses to remind me that I'd done the job right before and I could do it again.

It was a nice little confidence booster.

No harsh reprimand.

No-one was in trouble.

No judgement cast.

No excuses or blame.

The plate wasn't clean, so make it clean. Quite simple, it's a reject until it's no longer a reject.

All these years later, the REJECT principle still comes in handy. When you're thinking below the line there's

---

*When you're thinking
below the line there's
no need to punish
yourself.*

---

no need to punish yourself. Instead, accept that you wrestled with a below-the-line 'reject' thought and then choose to either repeat the thought or do your best to replace it with a boosting above-the-line thought.

ROC FUNDAMENTAL #6: THE 80:20 RULE

As humans we like to set targets and goals both big and small. Dinner by seven and assignment due on the seventh. It's good to have direction and deadlines, and feel like you're working towards something important.

ROC is no different. You need to set a realistic target for your mental fitness so you know what you're aiming for.

Allowing yourself to be below the line around 20% of your day, week and life (and accepting it) is both reasonable and realistic. It covers the times when you feel disappointed, cranky, worried, upset, flat, bored or even jealous. There could be times or circumstances in your life that put you below the line for more than 20% of the time. That's okay. Hearts can break, feelings can get hurt, dreams can be blown apart, and what you had in mind may not play out the way you planned.

Just remember that you have the strength, courage and love to help you to recover, reset and tiptoe your way back above the line at your own pace and in your own time.

Aiming to be above the line about 80% of your day, week and life is also reasonable and realistic. But while it's a good target, please don't think you need to stop at 80%. NO WAY! Go ahead and fly above the line as often as you can. Enjoy those 85%, 90%, 95% moments and 100% picture-perfect times, because your life will be full of them.

~~100%~~

AIM FOR 80%

Your above-the-line thoughts, heart talk, body talk and your behaviours and actions live here.

━━━━━━━━ YOUR CHOICE ━━━━━━━━

Your below-the-line thoughts, heart talk, body talk and your behaviours and actions live here.

AIM FOR 20%

~~0%~~

SHINE YOUR TORCH

I began writing this section just as the sun was rising. My house was mostly dark, but beams of light were creeping in.

I wandered into the kitchen to make a cuppa, and as I did the 2000-piece New York jigsaw puzzle we had been adding to over the past few weeks caught my eye. To my surprise, my husband had finished it off.

Done. Complete. Perfect.

Two thousand pieces in place and completely connected. It was awesome to see New York in all its glory.

But when I turned the light on I instantly noticed two pieces were missing. Two gaps. Two spaces. Two holes. Two empty places in the New York cityscape.

Deflated, I homed in on the imperfect jigsaw. I needed to check. I rotated the dimmer switch to shine more overhead light on the scene. Nope, the two pieces were still missing.

My coffee machine beeped, calling me back.

With the press of a button my cup was full, and for a moment it distracted me from the ruined jigsaw. Three weeks of building it piece by piece only to end up with an incomplete scene. So disappointing.

I wandered back to view the scene, hoping that by some miracle the two pieces had returned to take their place.

*Aiming to be
above the line about
80% of your day, week
and life is also reasonable
and realistic.*

And then it dawned on me. One thousand, nine hundred and ninety-eight pieces were in place. Two pieces were not.

For you ROCers who love numbers and data, it looked like this:

99.9% | 0.1%

My husband wandered into the room, and with great delight proclaimed that the jigsaw was finished. He loved that we could now see New York City, with the Empire State Building standing 443m tall from soil to tip.

He didn't mention the 0.1%. He wasn't even interested in the two pieces of blue sky that weren't there. Instead he told me of his dream to stand on the 102nd floor on the observation deck and take in a 360-degree view of New York City and beyond.

As you read my story, did you remember a moment in your life like the jigsaw moment in mine?

How often do you shine your torchlight on your own stuff-ups or things that didn't work out?

Do you remember making a mistake or a decision you regretted and, in forgetting to adjust your torchlight, this stopped you from moving onwards and upwards?

No city is perfect. No life is perfect. No family is perfect. But New York looks just as amazing with 1,998 pieces in place as it does with 2,000. One day we'll visit. And those two missing pieces won't stop that travel dream from coming true.

The ROC Recap – Section 1

Congratulations. Now you know the fundamentals of ROC.

Take them with you as you travel through the book, because every part of ROC and Rise hinges on them.

You now have the startup knowledge you need to read about resilience.

» Thoughts, feelings, emotions and actions are divided by the ROC line.

» Being below the line is part of natural human behaviour. It's just harder, heavier and pulls you down.

» Being above the line is also normal. It's just easier, lighter and lifts you up.

» You will experience both sides of the line over and over again.

» ROC blockers are thoughts, choices and actions that hold you back and hold you below the line.

» ROC boosters are things you can think, do and feel that help you move forward and help you to rise.

» Your thoughts have consequences. They affect your heart talk and body talk and the way you feel inside.

» You have a STUFF list. Everyone does. You choose how to think about everything on your list.

» Be kind to yourself. Don't judge yourself too harshly. It's okay to have 'reject' thoughts.

» Keep it real. Aim for 80:20. Aim to be up as much as you can. But remember, it's human nature to be below the line.

ROC, RISE and REPEAT

Notes & ROC Reminders

Take some time to reflect on what you've read in Section 1 about ROC Fundamentals. What caught your eye? What thoughts and ideas were triggered? What do you want to make sure you don't forget?

_____

_____

_____

_____

_____

_____

_____

_____

_____

_____

_____

_____

SECTION 2

ROAD TO RESILIENCE

ROAD TO RESILIENCE

I've asked teenagers to explain what resilience means to them. Here's what some of them said:

"When you can bounce back."

"The feeling you can recover from challenging situations."

"Believing in yourself so you can handle problems."

"Being humble and grateful."

"Pushing on when life feels hard."

"Not losing it and just giving up."

"To keep on going."

Resilience is a classic combination of all the thoughts, feelings, emotions and actions that help you recover, bounce back, dust yourself off and try again. But like most things you learn and practise in life, you need to do it in a way that feels right for you.

However, resilience doesn't come instantly. It takes time, work and patience.

You live in an Instant, Now and Immediate (INI) era where you can get a pizza delivered just by tapping on your phone. And it's pretty much all you've ever known.

Unfortunately, you can't transform yourself into a robust force and perfect model of resilience just by opening an app. Resilience can't be bought or sold, and it isn't a tangible item. But it can be enjoyed in your mind, held in your heart, and felt in your gut anywhere, anytime.

It's also powerful. It can help you handle the ups and downs, surprises and curve balls of school, sport, friendships, relationships and life. You can learn the skills you need to bounce back and recover when things go wrong.

Resilience is your rescue remedy. It helps you stand strong in the face of life's ups and downs.

You can raise your resilience level, but no-one else can do it for you.

And no human has the right to take it away from you.

No-one.

Ever.

Others might try to tamper with your resilience. But their efforts will be in vain, because you're both the gatekeeper and holder of the key.

RESILIENCE DOES	RESILIENCE DOES NOT
✓ Require good quality thinking	✗ Magically appear
✓ Feel great	
✓ Need to be practised	
✓ Come free	
✓ Take time to build	
✓ Help you to recover	
✓ Rely on your choices	
✓ Suit you	
✓ Look different for everyone	
✓ Call for bravery	
✓ Allow for 2nd, 3rd, 4th and 5th attempts	

Resilience can help you handle the ups and downs, surprises and curve balls of school, sport, friendships, relationships and life.

Which direction will you go?
Which adventure will you choose?
Ready. Set. Resilience.

NAME IT AND CLAIM IT

Not too long ago I was presenting to a group of Year Nine and Year Ten students.

While I was speaking, I noticed a guy sitting at the end of a long row at the back of the room. His body talk caught my attention. He was slouched, and looked miserable in every way.

The clock ticked over to 11 and the students began shuffling out for their morning break. As they did, the teacher in the room quietly called this young man over to him. I assumed he wanted to chat. Had he noticed the student's body talk too?

As I made my way towards the glass doors to take a break, I walked past the student and the teacher. They were talking back and forth, but the young guy looked so heavy hearted. His eyes were emotional and the teacher's eyes were full of concern.

The teacher then said a word that sent a chill down my spine: 'remorse'. It's a feeling of deep guilt and regret, and quite a heavy below-the-line thought.

The teacher put his hand on the student's shoulder and said, "Nick, you're feeling remorse, mate."

Nick stood motionless in a bubble of silence while he took it all in. He lifted his head ever so slightly, as if he had been thrown a life raft while swimming in deep and turbulent water.

Hearing the word 'remorse' seemed to lift the weight off Nick's shoulders. It didn't magically change the way he was feeling, but it went a long way to helping him recover.

Naming the revolting, intense below-the-line feeling consuming his mind, heart and body was exactly what he needed. It was as if time stood still when the word was spoken. The feeling had a name, and that somehow made it less frightening and confusing.

I don't know the story behind his remorse. But he had obviously messed up big time, and what he was experiencing was intense.

Has this happened to you?

If this happens again, try not to run and hide from the scary feelings and emotions rumbling through your body and mind. Instead, try leaning into the confusion and the weirdness of it all. This will help you remove the mystery behind the emotion.

Snatch back your power by naming and claiming it so you can be the one who decides your next move, whether it's below or above the line.

With his teacher's help, Nick named and claimed his emotion. And his relief was totally visible. His body talk was still hovering below the line, but that's to be expected. His below-the-line remorseful thoughts had activated his natural stress response system, and stress chemicals were flowing through his body. Unfortunately, these strong chemicals don't disappear the moment you name and claim the emotion. They need time to move through your body and drain away—a couple of hours sometimes.

So give yourself as much time as you need.

*Accept how you feel
right now and know it's
probably a temporary
feeling that will pass.*

RESILIENCE BOOSTER: NAME IT AND TRACE IT

Naming and writing down words that describe the feelings and emotions you're experiencing is a great way to own your heart talk without giving yourself a hard time.

» Give your emotions and feelings a name (e.g. angry, frustrated, jealous, overwhelmed).

» Accept it's how you feel right now and that it's probably a temporary feeling that will pass. (You'll find it easier to do the more you practise.)

» Trace your named feeling back to your original angry thought. You'll join the dots between angry thoughts and angry heart talk, which often leads to angry body talk.

» Switch anger for action. (I'll be talking more about this shortly.)

RESILIENCE BOOSTER: THE HARRY SHAKE

If you find yourself paralysed with fear, or totally overwhelmed with new and confusing emotions like Nick, the Harry Shake tool might be useful.

Harry is my loyal and much-loved Cocker Spaniel who is always around when I'm coaching. Perhaps you've met him.

He's also the dog with a tale about shaking when his walk in the park took an unexpected turn.

Harry was about eight months old, and we were strolling through the local park. As always, Harry was happily sniffing and wandering in and out of the bushes.

On this particular day a German Shepherd was also enjoying his walk. Harry was still a puppy, and we were mindful of his high-energy movements around adult dogs. His owner noticed our hesitation, but signalled that all was fine and we didn't need to worry. We walked on.

We were almost past the Shepherd when, without warning, he turned and launched himself at Harry. Using his massive body weight, he pinned Harry to the ground in a noisy and scary scuffle.

We reacted quickly, grabbing the dogs and pulling them apart. As soon as Harry was free we were out of there.

We did a body check to make sure he wasn't injured. Physically he was fine, but he was scared and so were we. Harry stayed close, but he was ruffled and reacting just like humans do—rattled, edgy and nervous. His stress system had been activated for sure.

But Harry soon took control of himself and did what dogs often do. He flung himself into a vigorous whole-body shake. His ears, tail, body and slobber jobber jaws were all in on the action, which lasted quite a while. Shake, shake, shake.

A dog's cleverness never ceases to amaze me. Harry's shake was his natural way of soothing himself after his intense ordeal.

It's how dogs release trapped emotions in their body. They shake it out. This instinctive soothing mechanism restores balance to their body, so they feel themselves again.

But it's not limited to dogs. It's equally effective for humans. If you feel a bit tense, stressed or overwhelmed, you may need to soothe yourself back into balance.

If Harry can shake it off, you can shake it off too.

*If you feel a bit tense,
stressed or overwhelmed,
you may need to soothe
yourself back into
balance.*

TRY THIS

Find a space where you can safely shake, jump and/or dance. Go wild for about 30 seconds (or whatever time feels right for you). Music can help too, so don't be afraid to shake it off to your favourite tune.

Next, take a couple of deep breaths. Breathe in deeply through your nose, and blow out through your mouth.

Now jump around, making sure to flick your arms, hands and fingers too. Imagine you're flicking out all of those below-the-line emotions. Sing and shout, just let it all out.

Now check. (We always check.)

How do you feel?

If there's still a ball of tension or stress trapped somewhere in your body hanging on for dear life, do it again.

Shake. REPEAT. Shake. REPEAT.

Harry was okay. He wasn't physically hurt. He stayed close and explored less, but that's to be expected when you've had a scare. But he still loved his park walks, and he was back exploring the bushes the very next day.

THE 6-WAY SWITCH

I spoke earlier about the need to accept or reject your thoughts without judgement. But there's a third option you can use to consciously take your thoughts from below the line to above the line: the 6-way switch.

But first, it's important to know you don't always have to switch. Depending on the STUFF that's come into your life it may be appropriate to sit for a while with those feelings and below-the-line thoughts zooming around in your mind.

So don't rush it, and don't let anyone else tell you you're moving too fast or too slow. How you move is entirely up to you.

But when you *are* ready to move, the 6-way switch is where you can choose to switch:

Doubts for Dreams
Anger for Action
Worries for Wishes
Fears for Freedom
Failure for Finding Out
Stress for Soothe

SWITCH DOUBTS FOR DREAMS

My dream was to bungee jump 216m from Bloukrans Bridge, which at the time was the highest bungee jump bridge in the world.

You might be thinking, "You did what?" I know. Crazy, right? But that's what dreams are about. They're personal, and that's the way they should be.

It's hard to believe that bungee jumping, one of my to-do-list dreams, began on Pentecost Island as an ancient tribal rite of passage ritual for boys becoming men.

Boys were called to leap from the highest point of two bamboo towers with vines attached to their ankles (which they prepared themselves, like my grandad prepared his own parachute). The aim was to leap off the tower and have the vines stop them before they touched the ground, avoiding injury and proving their manhood.

(I wonder if they look at modern-day bungee jumping and wonder what all the fuss is about.)

Back to my dream. We climbed the internal steps of the huge concrete bridge to the top, where we were harnessed and clicked into the pendulum bungee technology. That's where I met Seb and Miguel—tourists from

Would his dream have come true if he switched his thoughts away from his doubt and towards his dream?

Spain who, like me, were ready to make their bungee jump dreams come alive. They were pumped, with their eyes firmly fixed on their boyhood dreams.

Strapped in, we were ready.

The beat of loud music thumped through the concrete and filled the vast valley below. With adrenaline flowing and high-fives all round, we nominated to leap from the bridge one by one. (It was a volunteer thing.)

I remember peering over the edge. My heart was beating so hard I wondered if it would explode out of my chest.

Miguel stepped up first. He was ready. He took his position on the jump mat, and after completing the safety check he jumped. He did it. He lived his dream.

Seb was next, and he got the 'thumbs up' from the bungee jumping team. We waited and watched. But Seb remained still. Observing his body talk, it was clear that doubtful, dream crushing thoughts had moved in.

We waited. Minutes passed. He stepped back from the jump mat.

"No jump," the safety crew called out.

I watched and wondered. Would his dream have come true if he switched his thoughts away from his doubt and towards his dream? I guess I'll never know.

Have your doubting thoughts ever become so loud that your most precious dreams were lost in the noise, drowned out and forgotten?

Then it was my turn. Like a penguin, I shuffled my tightly strapped feet towards the jump platform on the edge of the bridge. I was clicked in by the team, secured and ready to leap. The jumping rules were repeated: head up, back arched and arms out wide.

"On my count. Three, two, one, jump!"

I had doubts. Of course I did. But I took them with me as I jumped. I flew out over the valley below, plummeting into silent air space. Time stood still as gravity took hold. I made my bungee dream come true.

Whatever your dream …
Love it. Dream it. Google it. Imagine it.
Believe in it. Talk about it. Plan for it.
Create it. Chase it. Own it.
Don't let doubts damage your dreams.

Listen closely to the thoughts that push you forward, lift you up and hold you tight, so you can follow your dreams and pursue everything that's important to you.

RESILIENCE BOOSTER: DREAM BIG

Don't let your doubts damage your dreams.

Spill your dreams here. No matter how big or small they are, bare them all.

Your 'Do it now' dreams.

_____

_____

_____

_____

Your 'Do it soon rather than later' dreams.

_____

_____

_____

_____

Your 'Do it later' dreams.

_____

_____

_____

_____

*Listen closely to the
thoughts that push you
forward, lift you up and
hold you tight.*

Your 'Do it in your lifetime' dreams.

_____

_____

_____

TURN YOUR DREAMS INTO REALITY

Choose three of your dreams. Now, brainstorm all the ways you can make them happen. (Need more space? There are extra pages at the back of this book.)

Dream 1 _____

Road to reality _____

_____

Dream 2 _____

Road to reality _____

_____

Dream 3 _____

Road to reality _____

_____

Choose your own adventure. Start with your dreams. Make them happen.

SWITCH ANGER FOR ACTION

Have you ever felt angry? *Really* angry? You're not alone.

Let's get one thing straight: anger is a completely normal human emotion. It's one of the hundreds of emotions you'll experience in your lifetime. It's a damn powerful emotion, but it's not pretty. And it's definitely one that can catch you by surprise and take your emotions from zero to sky high in seconds.

This might explain the huge social trend to hide angry thoughts and feelings and push them away. (Fortunately, it's changing now.) Anger can spark rage in your head and a blazing fire in your belly like no other emotion can.

Anger is normal. But it can also be a tip-top ROC blocker.

Anger shows up in different people for different reasons. You might respond angrily to some STUFF, but not to other STUFF. You may feel angry when you sense injustice or unfairness, or you're publicly embarrassed or wronged in a way you can't explain.

Some of the words on your STUFF list (page 73) may also trigger an angry response in you. Remember to name it and claim it when it pops in.

When it shows up, you don't need to have all the words to explain it. You're young, and your body often does the talking for you.

Don't feel embarrassed or ashamed of your angry thoughts. It just adds another layer to anger and drags you further and further below the line. Anger is usually a temporary emotion, which means it will come and go. But you need to give it time to come and go.

It may feel permanent when it swarms your head, heart and body like angry bees defending their hive. But this is your body's natural stress response system doing its job to protect you and keep you safe.

I asked teenagers to tell me the STUFF that wound them up and triggered anger in their head, heart and body. As you read the list, you might feel a little angry too. Then again, you might not. That's the thing about STUFF: it means different things to everyone.

Here's what they said.

Cruelty to animals, bullying,
disease and serious medical conditions,
seeing fights and violence,
people being treated unfairly,
war and violence, discrimination,
racism, environmental neglect,
people being left out, public put-downs,
gossip, crime.

*When anger shows up,
your body's natural
stress response system
fires up too.*

RESILIENCE BOOSTER: PUT ENERGY INTO ACTION

When anger shows up, your body's natural stress response system fires up too. Your brain thinks you're in danger, so it pumps stress chemicals (adrenaline and cortisol) through your body. And as you now know, this puts you on high alert because it's trying to keep you safe from danger—real or imagined.

Yes, it's a clever natural defence system that has kept humans alive for a very long time. But while it's handy if you're being chased by a cheetah, it can get a little carried away with itself in our modern world (assuming you don't have to worry about cheetahs in your street).

Very few people enjoy feeling angry because it can stick around for hours, sometimes days.

Anger can also show up in your behaviour, with you:

» overreacting and blowing things way out of proportion

» yelling, screaming and swearing

» saying things you don't mean (either face-to-face or on social media)

» physically hitting and hurting

» damaging property

» making decisions you wouldn't normally make.

Take a moment to reflect on the STUFF that's happening in your life now.

What triggers an angry reaction within you? Don't judge it. Just write it.

_____

_____

_____

_____

_____

Choose one word from the list and write it here. This is the STUFF that triggers an angry reaction.

_____

Now write your thoughts here.

_____

_____

_____

_____

_____

Do you notice these thoughts making your heart talk?

Write your heart talk here.

_____

_____

_____

_____

_____

_____

How does your body talk when you think angry thoughts? (If you need a reminder of how your body talks (sweaty palms, clenched jaw, tight tummy, shaking, headaches, tears, etc.) take another look at page 62.)

Write your body talk here.

_____

_____

_____

_____

_____

_____

*What do you do when
you're forced to take
full responsibility for
yourself and own your
actions—the good, the
bad and the wacky?*

You're almost there. This is an opportunity to pay attention to your own behaviours when you're in the angry zone. This is a big deal, because I'm asking you to observe yourself when you're probably not at your best. No-one really enjoys this stage. But this small task is the powerhouse of your ROCability. You're forced to take full responsibility for yourself and own your actions—the good, the bad and the wacky.

What do you do? How do you behave? (Do you shout, slam doors, say unkind things?)

Write your angry actions here.

_____

_____

_____

_____

_____

_____

It's important to know everything you wrote is okay.

Your honesty and bravery give you the chance to choose your own adventure.

TIP: *Staying in the angry zone for too long uses way too much energy. It's like running a marathon you haven't done any training for. In fact, it's worse. At least with a marathon you can record your personal best. Emerging from the angry zone leaves you emotionally exhausted, upset, and often filled with regret. And there's rarely any reward.*

LET'S SUMMARISE

The STUFF that triggered an angry reaction in you is:

_____

_____

Your thoughts are: **angry**

Your heart talk: _____

Your body talk: _____

You act/behave by: _____

Does this pattern help you to rise above the line or fall below the line?   Rise   Fall

Most people say anger pulls them further below the line. It even attracts more below-the-line thoughts and emotions such as regret, frustration, annoyance and rage.

That's one big mix of toxic doom and gloom.

So here's my question: if you didn't respond to STUFF by using anger, what alternative *action* could you take to empower you?

Above-the-line *action* redirects your energy, fills your heart and mind with positive purpose, and helps you to shift gear. Taking action instead of displaying anger lifts your spirits and changes your focus.

Here's what switching anger for action could look like.

CRUELTY TO ANIMALS – Put your energy into loving and caring for animals. Be around them, volunteer to work with them, or think about a career in animal health. Be with people who share your love for animals.

BULLYING – Put your energy into including people, welcoming new kids and being nice. Look out for anyone being hassled and simply lead by example with your kindness and care. Speak up and tell an adult who can help if necessary. Hang out with people who share your friendship values.

*Above-the-line
action redirects your
energy and helps you to
shift gear.*

In your day-to-day life, how could you switch feelings of anger for action?

Remember, this doesn't mean anger totally disappears. That's fake and unrealistic. But by intentionally switching you can shift your focus and energy to line up with the 80:20 rule—80% action, 20% anger.

Note some ways you can turn anger into action below:

ANGER	ACTION

Make the switch to keep yourself mentally fit and protect your ROC level.

SWITCH WORRIES FOR WISHES

Your worries are real. Everyone has them, and it's normal to worry now and then. Rest easy knowing you're not alone.

Yes, it helps to know you're not alone. But hearing stories of other people's worries doesn't always help you reign in your own worrying thoughts.

Let's face it: worrying thoughts are first-class ROC blockers. So you need practical alternatives to worrying. You've probably heard words of wisdom such as, "Just don't worry about it" or "What's the worst thing that can happen?" Unfortunately, they're not always effective when you're stuck in a worry well and struggling to step out. You need other ways to step out.

Most of the time you're probably worrying about something on your STUFF list (page 73). Chances are you've got a lot going on in your life, and as you get older your STUFF list gets longer.

But that doesn't mean your worry list needs to get longer.

Worry sucks the joy out of life. It's like wearing a rain jacket in summer and waiting for the torrential rain to come.

Worrying can look and sound different for everyone. But there seems to be a common ROC blocking trifecta that goes like this:

1. Think about anything that could go wrong.
2. Replay the worst possible scenarios in your mind.
3. Constantly talk about the stuff you fear the most.

If you've fallen into the worry well before, don't panic. We all do it. You've done it before, and you'll do it again because no-one is immune to the one-two-three trifecta. But be aware it has the power to pull you down below the line and keep you totally worry-struck.

On the next page is the ROC booster I share with all worried teenagers.

Your worries are real.
Everyone has them,
and it's normal to
worry now and then.

RESILIENCE BOOSTER: WORRY LESS, WISH MORE

STEP ONE — CHOOSE YOUR #1 WORRY

What item on your STUFF list are you worrying about right now? You might have a few, but for now just choose one. (You can come back and use this booster to help with your other worries later.)

_____

_____

_____

_____

_____

STEP TWO — ONE-MINUTE WORRY

ROC is being real and honest about what's going on.

There's something on your mind that's bothering you, and you're worrying about it.

Here's your chance to get your wildest worry thoughts out of your head, heart and body—whatever you think could go wrong, fall apart, fail miserably, not work out or end in disaster.

Set the timer on your phone for 60 seconds, and dive into your worry well.

(When you try this for the first time, you could be tempted to burst the time limit. Don't. Just don't. One minute is enough.)

One minute writing in the worry well. Let's do it. Go.

_____

_____

_____

_____

_____

_____

_____

_____

_____

_____

60, 59, 58, 57, 56 ... 33 ... 19 ... 11 ... 5, 4, 3, 2, 1.

You're done.

STEP THREE – HEART CHECK

Now's a good time to check how your heart feels. You've been in your worry well for 60 seconds, thinking and writing below-the-line worries.

Do you feel better or worse? _____

What's your heart saying to you?

_____

_____

_____

_____

STEP FOUR – BODY CHECK

You know your body sensations reflect your inner thoughts and emotions. Take a moment to notice your body talk. What's it saying to you?

_____

_____

_____

_____

_____

*Your body sensations
reflect your inward
thoughts and
emotions.*

Nice work. You've completed steps one through four. Now you have a decision to make.

OPTION 1 – KEEP WORRYING

Stay in the worry well. This will trigger your body's natural stress response system to fire up.

Let fear, anxiousness, catastrophic and nervous thoughts dive in with you.

Repeat, repeat, repeat.

Spiral down, down, down.

Get stuck in the well.

Worry about getting stuck in the well.

Repeat, repeat, repeat.

Spiral down, down, down.

Worry about being stuck, repeating and spiralling.

OPTION 2 – START WISHING (my preference)

Wishing is not pretending the problem isn't there.

Wishing is not sticking your head in the sand like an emu.

Wishing is not denying reality.

Wishing is making the decision to replace a worrying thought with a wishful thought.

Why?

Wishing thoughts help soothe your body's natural stress response so you can feel less stressed, less anxious and far less frantic. It can make you feel calmer, more settled and happier in your own skin.

Here are a few of my favourite wish-over-worry switches.

> **"I hope everyone arrives on time and we have a great night"** (rather than "I'm worried everyone will be late and I'll be there on my own").

> **"I want to be selected and I'll keep doing my best so I'm in with a chance"** (rather than "I'm worried my name won't be on the list and I'll miss out").

> **"In my mind I can picture the party going well, with everyone getting along and having fun"** (rather than "I'm so worried there will be drama at the party and no-one will want to stay").

> **"I'm sure that once I start the test I'll remember what I studied and be ready to write"** (rather than "I'm so worried I'll freeze when I see the questions and won't know what to write").

Think back to the worry thought you cracked wide open.

Your original worry: _____

_____

_____

_____

_____

Switch it: _____

_____

_____

_____

Instead of worrying about what could go wrong, think about what could go right. That's a lot more fun.

When you make the switch, you feel mentally fit and enjoy more time on the bright side.

*Fear is a natural
survival instinct you need
to keep you safe.*

SWITCH FEARS FOR FREEDOM

Fear is a powerful below-the-line human emotion most people experience from time to time. Your fears can seem totally real.

Fear is a natural survival instinct you need to keep you safe. Sometimes you're totally aware of the fearful thoughts rising within you, so you practise naming it and claiming it.

But sometimes it feels like a high-speed freight train has rammed you from behind. You didn't see it coming. It hits with a thud.

Fear of failure. Fear of success.
Fear of not fitting in.
Fear of standing out.
Fear of not being liked.
Fear of pressure.
Fear of exclusion.
Fear of not being good enough.
Fear of not being in control.
Fear of being alone.
Fear of losing. Fear of fear.

Teenagers often talk to me about fear. Like you, they want the skills to handle it when it shows up and the tools to recover from it when it starts taking over, strangling their confidence when they need it the most.

While fear is a natural human response, it can sometimes rise up at the most inappropriate and inconvenient times. Ever felt overwhelmed with fear when entering a room full of people, at a party, or checking your exam results online? You probably noticed the fear thudding through your heart and body long before your below-the-line fearful thoughts.

When your thoughts plunge down below the line, your body activates its natural fight, flee or freeze response. You think you're in danger, so your body produces adrenaline and cortisol. This surge of hormones triggers a hyper-sensitive reaction within you. Your muscles fire up, and you may well:

- » get the heck out of there (flee)
- » stay and face the fear head on (fight)
- » become stuck and remain stationary (freeze).

This is normal, and good to know.

On the flipside, it's not so great if you're just trying to be a teenager going to parties, playing sport, meeting new people, doing tests and trying to fit in.

When fear shows up without an invitation
it feels real and revolting.
It fires you up with feisty chemicals.
It makes you do the weirdest stuff.
It can block you from being yourself.

Fear can keep you stuck, frozen and unable to move.

Fear can stop you believing and dreaming.

Fear can block you from trying new things, meeting friends, and saying yes to challenges that are perfect for you.

And we in turn can choose to block them.

Blocking those below-the-line fearful feelings is one way to handle them. But most teenagers say it loses its effectiveness and doesn't work after a while. Numbing, avoiding and ignoring can be handy shortcuts, but they don't cut it when life gets serious, challenges pop up and opportunities arise.

Why?

Shortcuts can help you feel better in the short term. However, they rarely work in the long term—especially when you're working your butt off to ROC and rise in your teenage years and beyond.

The ROC way is to understand your fear, and let it teach you rather than trap you.

The ROC way is to understand your fear, and let it teach you rather than trap you.

Be the grand optimist, not the world's loudest pessimist.

RESILIENCE BOOSTER: GET FRIENDLY WITH FEAR

You probably feel fear in your body before you understand it in your mind. Fear is normal.

Fear shows up like a loud knock at the door when you've just settled in to watch a movie. Don't ignore the knock of fear. Answer it. It could be delivering an important message for you.

Press pause and open the door. It's a messenger delivering a letter.

Whenever fear turns up, follow these instructions:

1. Notice your body talk. It will let you know if fear has flooded your thoughts.

2. Take a big deep breath and ask yourself:

What is this feeling in my body? Does this feeling have a name (e.g. worry, dread, concern, doubt)? Name it and claim it: _____

_____

What am I fearful of? (e.g. Being embarrassed, failing, being alone, getting it wrong, standing out.)

_____

3. Is my fearful thought lifting me up or dragging me down?

_____

4. Name and claim the above-the-line thought you'd like to think instead of the fearful thought (e.g. I am **calm**, I **trust** myself, **I can** do this, I am **capable**).

_____

_____

The aim is not to become fear_less_, but rather to make your next move _despite the fear._

Feel the fear and forge ahead on the road to freedom.

SWITCH FAILURE FOR FINDING OUT

In my mind, failure is one of the best and most educational inventions ever made by humans. You're probably frowning in disbelief because you know as well as I do that failure lives below the line and feels absolutely revolting. Failing can be so embarrassing, especially when you don't achieve your goals or other people are expecting big things from you.

No-one really likes talking about failure, so you might be tempted to skip this section and flick ahead. But I encourage you to stick with me, because you'll learn how to switch your thoughts from failure to finding out—something I wish I knew how to do when I was a teenager.

Some of the most accomplished humans failed before they succeeded. You've no doubt heard all the JK Rowling 'rags to riches' stories, and how many potentially game-winning shots Michael Jordan has missed. They both pushed through repeated failures to make their dreams come true. High fives to them.

With so many ways to fail, there's a good chance you'll experience failure many times in your life. And when you do, it will challenge and test your mental fitness in ways you never thought possible.

*Keep in mind that
'failing' is different
for everyone.*

But that's okay. You're human. It's pretty much expected.

According to teenagers I've spoken to, failure can look like this:

- ✓ Not selected in the team
- ✓ A relationship breaking up
- ✓ Getting detention
- ✓ Not passing a test
- ✓ Forgetting information
- ✓ Letting the team down
- ✓ Missing lines in a play
- ✓ Not reaching your PB
- ✓ Breaking something
- ✓ Falling out with friends
- ✓ Coming second. Not first
- ✓ Losing top spot
- ✓ B, C, D result at school
- ✓ Mucking up a speech
- ✓ Losing your temper
- ✓ Turning up late
- ✓ Breaking a rule
- ✓ Losing your race
- ✓ Dropping a catch
- ✓ Missing the winning goal
- ✓ Getting in trouble
- ✓ Letting a friend down
- ✓ Not being accepted
- ✓ Being rejected
- ✓ Losing your job
- ✓ Making a poor decision
- ✓ Losing. Not winning
- ✓ Not invited to an event

Keep in mind that 'failing' is different for everyone. Some examples will feel true for you, while others won't feel true at all. Once again, that's the nature of STUFF.

Failure can bring on a range of emotions—sadness, frustration, anger, disappointment, and so on. If you feel any of these emotions because you think you've failed, dive right in and do those emotions well. Dedicate time to them, give them everything you've got and *really* cry, throw a tantrum (in a safe way of course), sulk or whatever it is you need to do.

This is important, so don't skip it. Why? Because ignored thoughts, feelings and emotions usually come back to bite you in the bum further down the track.

Your honesty is an important part of making the switch from failing to finding out.

Finding out is not ignoring your apparent shortfall, the lesser score, the unexpected result or the words you didn't want to hear. You can't change a score or the message in a text.

But you can change how you think about these things.

To do this, you're invited to take part in a fact-finding mission that will make failure your most trusted and helpful teacher.

RESILIENCE BOOSTER: GET CURIOUS

Whenever failure strikes, go on a fact-finding mission to find out more. When you reflect (which is a top-class above-the-line habit to get into) you put yourself in the best possible position to learn from failure.

DO THIS:

» Acknowledge what worked well for you, even though you failed.

» Ask for feedback from your trusted crew so you can make changes next time.

» Think about your original goal. Was it realistic and achievable, or a crazy pipe dream?

» Be honest. Did you take any shortcuts along the way?

» Do you need additional help or skills? If you do, what do you need and how will you get it?

» Are you on a path that's right for you? Will you keep going or change direction?

» Were you prepared? Would you change it up if you did it all over again?

» Did something completely out of your control happen that blocked you or stopped you?

If failure is a false start, then give yourself permission to tweak so you can try again.

I tell myself this. False starts happen. They're a part of life. If failure is a false start, then give yourself permission to correct, adjust, tweak or refine so you can try again.

Of course, you always have a choice.

*You can stop, give up, or head
in a different direction.*

You always have a choice. You can wait around for things to change, or you can make the changes that keep you ROCing your way.

SWITCH STRESS FOR SOOTHE

The first thing I want you to know about stress is that it's completely normal. The second thing I want you to know is stress can either work for you or against you. It's your choice for stress to be a booster or a blocker.

STRESS AS A BOOSTER

Soothing above-the-line thoughts can prompt your nervous system to give you a *little surge of adrenaline and cortisol.* That short and sharp burst of energy can then galvanise you into much-needed action. For example:

Thought: I've got 30 minutes to get this assignment done before netball training. If I put my head down and concentrate, it can be done and dusted before I go.

Action: You get started and make the best possible use of your available time.

STRESS AS A BLOCKER

Below-the-line thoughts trigger a *massive and ongoing release of adrenaline and cortisol,* which creates a gross feeling of overwhelm and pressure that makes you crumble into a stressed-out heap. This level of stress also messes with your mental fitness and makes you behave out of character. For example:

Thought: Geez, I've only got 30 minutes left to get this stupid assignment done, I'll never get it finished. It's impossible. It's too hard. Far out, I don't even know where to start. I'm going to be late for training. How embarrassing will that be?

Action: You stall, procrastinate and pummel yourself with more below-the-line thoughts. You give up and walk away. Assignment incomplete.

IMPORTANT NOTE: Repeatedly blocking stress can negatively affect your sleep patterns, what you choose to eat and drink, your friendships, and how you use social media. And here's the kicker: it also affects how you think and feel about yourself, your life and your future. It can mess with your mind, your heart and your body.

Sound familiar?

It's time to look blocking stress right between the eyes. I'm not suggesting you try to remove all the feelings of stress from your life because I don't believe that's realistic (or even possible).

But I will suggest that while you probably can't change the stuff you're stressing about, you *can* change how you think about it.

Practise shifting your attention away from stressful thoughts and towards soothing thoughts.

Stressful thoughts increase your chance of falling below the line.

Soothing thoughts increase your chance of rising above the line.

Practise shifting your attention away from stressful thoughts and towards soothing thoughts.

Here are two handy questions you can ask yourself whenever a stressful thought turns up:

Does this stressful thought help me ROC?

_____

Is there a soothing thought I can think instead?

_____

A great way to practise coping with stressful situations is to put yourself in stressful or potentially intense situations. Yes, you read that correctly. _Go to the stress._ Don't run away from it. Every time you avoid a stressful situation, you miss out on an opportunity to learn how to manage yourself and your stress levels. You don't have to go searching for stress. But you can choose to stay and learn from it rather than run and hide.

Stress less. Soothe more.

RESILIENCE BOOSTER: SOOTHING ROC BREATH

The ROC breath is your soothing booster that's always available. It's especially useful when you're trying to choose soothing thoughts over stressful thoughts.

Resetting yourself with soothing ROC breaths can interrupt below-the-line thoughts from gathering momentum, giving your nervous system the chance to reset and be at ease.

Soothing ROC breaths will boost you and help melt your stress away.

TRY THIS:

Deeply inhale fresh air through your nose and into your belly. As you do, close your eyes and imagine your soothing breaths inflating your lungs and your belly to capacity. (Place your hands on your chest and tummy so you can feel your body breathing.)

Gently hold your breath for a few seconds (or whatever length of time is comfortable for you).

Breathe out through your mouth as if you're slowly but strongly blowing out candles on a cake. Notice your lungs emptying and your chest and belly dropping as you exhale.

As you exhale, picture any stressful thoughts being carried away in the wind. See them rise, fly away and disappear in the distance.

Keep doing this until you feel lighter. Practise often. It's a simple boosting and soothing tool you can use whenever you need it.

Blowing out stress creates more space for the soothing, compassionate, kind and caring thoughts that help you to ROC and rise.

TIP: *Soothe and Shake.*
Combine soothing ROC breaths with
the Harry Shake for the ultimate
boost and stress release.

Your inner control freak
tries to hijack your
happiness with
stealth–like accuracy.

RESILIENCE BOOSTER: CATCH THE CONTROL FREAK

Have you ever tried boosting your resilience by controlling the stuff that's happening in your life?

Your inner control freak tries to hijack your happiness with stealth-like accuracy. It sneaks into your world on a mission to be across everything, create perfection at every corner, and leave no room for error. Control usually leaves a dirty trail of anxious, stressed and worried thinking that blocks you from going with the flow at school, at home and when you're out and about for the day.

Here are a few classic signs the inner control freak is trying to ... well, control your life:

» over-planning a catch-up with your friends

» organising every second of your day (or your friend's day)

» future forecasting—trying to make sure the next five years are totally sorted with absolutely no surprises, changes, cancellations or spontaneity

» always a plan in place, as well as a backup plan in case the first plan doesn't go to plan

It's exhausting.

If you're cringing as you read this because the tiny voice inside your head is whispering, "Oh no, that's totally me," don't panic. That used to be me too—a control freak trying to force everything rather than letting it flow.

But then I realised how my ROC blocking habit was exhausting me. I consoled myself that it wasn't such a bad thing because a control freak's intentions are usually good. They just want life to work out the right way (whatever that means) so everyone and everything is happy and well. But rather than guiding it and letting it flow, they force it, force it and force it some more. You know where this force habit resides, don't you? Yep, well and truly below the line.

Goodbye force. Hello flow.
Less force. More flow.

YOU CAN CONTROL	YOU CANNOT CONTROL
✓ Your thoughts	✗ Anything that is not YOU
✓ Your emotions	
✓ Your feelings	
✓ Your choices (big and small)	
✓ Your behaviours	
✓ Your sleep routine	
✓ Your food selection	
✓ Your movement and exercise	
✓ Your self-talk	
✓ Your heart talk	
✓ Your body talk	
✓ Your attitude	
✓ Your choice to ask for help	

*The only thing
you can really
control is you.*

If you hold on tight to the stuff you can't control, you're bound to feel more stressed, anxious and overwhelmed. You might even be tempted to hold on extra tight rather than loosening your grip so you can go with the flow.

So much of your life is out of your control. Rain falls, and your plans are lost to the weather. The train arrives late, ruining your schedule. The cricket umpire points his index finger to the sky, and your time at the crease is over.

The only thing you can really control is you.

But that's good, because it means you can choose how you think about and respond to the rain, the train and the umpire's call.

TIP: *When the control freak in me starts to flex its muscle (which it does from time to time), I repeat this little mantra in my mind. DON'T FORCE, JUST FLOW.*

The Resilience Recap — Section 2

You've probably noticed that whenever you switch and use a resilience booster you're raising your resilience and building your mental fitness. The habits you practise on your good days and your bad days will help you handle life's ups and downs more easily and naturally.

Now that you've added to your selection of resilience boosting tools, you're invited to take the 10-Day Road to Resilience Challenge.

YOUR 10-DAY ROAD TO RESILIENCE

Each day, pick a switch or booster. Have a go at incorporating it into different parts of your life—parties, classes at school, recess and lunch breaks, friendships and even at home. Test them out and notice how they all add value to your ROCability.

1. **Name it and Claim it** – This makes feelings less overwhelming and mysterious.

2. **Name it and Trace it** – So you can see the connection between your thoughts and your heart talk.

3. **Harry Shake** – A great way to shake it out and let go of below-the-line emotions trapped in your body.

4. **Switch Doubts for Dreams** – Make your dream thoughts louder and prouder than doubting thoughts.

5. **Switch Anger for Action** – Use your energy to take action in an above-the-line way.

6. **Switch Worries for Wishes** – Focus your thoughts on what you want to happen.

7. **Switch Fear for Freedom** – Don't aim to be fearless. Aim to make your move in the presence of fear.

8. **Switch Failure for Finding Out** – Let failure be your teacher and tour guide as you reset and try again.

9. **Switch Stress for Soothe** – A little stress isn't bad, but a lot of stress is. When stress shows up, choose to soothe.

10. **Catch the Control Freak** – Flow, don't force. Give yourself permission to be surprised on life's rollercoaster ride.

Notes & ROC Reminders

Take some time to reflect on what you've read in Section 2 about resilience. What caught your eye? What thoughts and ideas were triggered? What do you want to make sure you don't forget?

_____

_____

_____

_____

_____

_____

_____

_____

_____

_____

_____

_____

_____

SECTION 3

BRIGHT SIDE OPTIMISM

BRIGHT SIDE OPTIMISM

Who doesn't love spending time with an optimist? The person at school, on your team or at home who plays the game of life on the bright side. You might know someone who lives optimistically. Their attitude, actions and conversations are full of hope and positivity, and they believe good things will happen both now and in the future.

There are so many advantages to living optimistically rather than pessimistically (which is living on the dull side of life believing nothing will work out well and the future isn't brightly lit).

Optimists don't stick their head in the sand like an emu to avoid life's realities. Instead they:

> » challenge their own thoughts (especially when they're below the line) and choose to either stay

there or work their way back above the line

» look for the good in situations, even if they have to dig deep to find it

» persist more and give up less easily. This is their choice—it doesn't just 'happen' to them

» see setbacks as bumps in the road and an opportunity to find another way. (But they still feel the heartache of failure and loss, and need time to recover.)

» stress less, flow more. They practise this because it's an easier way to live.

Now more than ever, building a sense of optimism helps you handle the sharp bends, unexpected twists and extreme highs and lows of your teenage rollercoaster ride.

OPTIMISM IS

- ✓ Glass half full thinking
- ✓ Helpful in stressful situations
- ✓ The opposite of pessimism
- ✓ Something you can learn and practise
- ✓ Believing in the good
- ✓ A good feeling you create
- ✓ An attitude of choice
- ✓ A habit that takes time to build and master
- ✓ A lighter, brighter and easier way to think and feel about your life

OPTIMISM IS NOT

- ✗ Instant or immediate
- ✗ Always easy
- ✗ A perfect life
- ✗ Ignoring problems and challenges
- ✗ An attitude that can be outsourced
- ✗ A quick fix
- ✗ A habit that you can learn overnight
- ✗ Pretending problems don't exist
- ✗ Glass half empty thinking

The ROC equivalent of UNO's wild card is the wish word 'yet'.

THE ROC WISH WORD: 'YET'

Optimism is built around positivity and hopeful expectation, which is why I want to introduce you to Renae, who was desperate to pass her Practical Driving Assessment Test.

After two unsuccessful attempts, Renae had plunged below the line. Her thundering thoughts were chipping away at her ROC level. She'd started talking herself out of passing her next test, and her optimistic attitude was sliding fast.

In our coaching session I listened to her falling thoughts, which were doing their best to stick. It was the perfect time to talk about UNO, the card game of colour and tactics.

"Do you remember playing UNO?"

With a smile Renae remembered, thinking back to camping trips and long car rides.

I reminded Renae of UNO's secret weapon and ultimate game changer—the wild card. This card gives whoever uses it the power to choose whatever colour they like, and often leads to victory.

And then I told her about the ROC equivalent of UNO's wild card—the wish word 'yet'.

'Yet' gives you the power to change your thoughts and your life, just as the wild card lets you change the colour in a game of UNO.

This **ever-reliable ROC wish word** holds a place in time for you. It helps you see beyond what hasn't gone to plan and to all the great things that haven't even happened yet.

So Renae hadn't passed her test **yet**. This single word lifted her thoughts into a higher place of hope and possibility. It reminded her that while she hadn't passed yet, with lessons and driving hours and an above-the-line attitude, she will pass soon.

This little wish word is coated with confidence and has the muscle power to propel you back above the line where you belong.

When our coaching conversation was complete, Renae took the wish word with her. And you guessed it: on attempt number three she passed her driving test.

Add the word 'yet' to your thoughts. It's a ROC-boosting habit you can practise instantly. Without too much effort, you'll be adding 'yet' to everything you think and say. And you'll notice how good it feels when you do.

Want an instant boost? Just add 'yet'. It opens the gates of possibility.

THE ROC 5

While holidaying in Hawaii a couple of years ago, my son and I talked about how crazy it was to be standing on a volcanic island in the middle of the Pacific Ocean.

It was April. The skies were blue, the water was still, and the Honolulu sand stretched as far as the eye could see.

There was a buzz of happiness in the air. And it was more than just holiday happiness. It was a 'we're loving every moment of life' kind of happiness. I'd say it was a 100% moment. (Ever felt so above the line you could almost touch the clouds? It was like that.)

Everyone was smiling and saying "Aloha". In Hawaiian culture it means both "Hello" and "Goodbye", but also speaks of compassion, kindness, love and peace. Such a beautiful word.

As we walked along the beach, a local walked towards us wearing a bright yellow t-shirt. Of course there's nothing unusual about that. But as he got closer the words written across his chest came into focus.

"Live like it's New Year's Day."

After reading those words I couldn't help but smile. It reminded me of the excitement I feel waking up on the first day of a brand new year. I love it.

Want an instant boost?
Just add 'yet'. It opens the
gates of possibility.

It's not so much because it's the traditional day of goals and resolutions, but because it can set the scene for new beginnings, changing thoughts or different routines in anyone's life.

It's simple. It's personal. It's powerful.

The words on his shirt pulled me in. I was intrigued, and wanted to understand why. I was doing my best to live like it was New Year's Day, but what did that mean exactly?

In my mind, five standout ROC habits can help us live like it's New Year's Day:

BE CURIOUS
BE HOPEFUL
BE PRESENT
BE QUIET
BE GRATEFUL

BE CURIOUS (BE NIELE)

Curiosity is a top-class optimism booster.

In Hawaii, the word for curious is *niele* (pronounced 'knee eh lay'), so I'm guessing that Hawaiian guy wearing the t-shirt was onto something.

When you're curious you:

> » are open minded, and thus more able to learn and hold onto information

> » feel the flow and your confidence grows in new or unfamiliar situations

> » relax, so your creative juices can flow and you can come up with cool ideas

> » are present—right here, right now.

Curious thinking is a natural optimism booster, especially when you receive feedback or think you're being criticised. Curious thinking shakes off optimism blockers—that defensive, protective and over-sensitive thinking that shows up in your mind from time to time.

Being curious enhances your mental fitness, pushes you into a world of possibility, and lifts you above the line in a New Year's Day kind of way.

BE HOPEFUL (MANAOLANA)

Hope is a vital optimism booster. It's a self-made feeling that keeps you buoyant, wishing and believing, and gushes with expectation that something good could come your way.

When I think about it, that t-shirt guy's chest was inundated with hope for the future. And it was certainly a reminder to persevere and keep your motivation candle burning.

Whenever I ask teenagers to define hope, they say words like 'dream', 'wish' and 'faith'. There's no right or wrong answer—how you experience hope is personal. In Hawaii, 'hope' translates to *manaolana*. Some children are even named Mana'olana. How cool is that? You would literally be hope with a heartbeat.

Hope shuts the door on annoying doom and gloom blockers that try to dominate your thoughts when life isn't going your way and you can't even buy your own luck.

Hope doesn't bring any guarantees for the future. But it sure can lift your spirits and keep you inspired to do your best. It keeps the doors of opportunity open (even if only slightly), because the alternative is rather boring and beige.

The impossible will start to feel possible when you spend more time hanging out with other hopeful ROCers.

Hope serves as a reminder that your goal is 80:20 living so you can keep your eye on the target. Change is possible, good news is coming, and happy endings and silver linings are within reach.

TIP — *To feel hopeful, surround yourself with people who are optimistic, have hopeful conversations, and purposefully look on the bright side of life (e.g. your dream team and your crew).*

Watch out. Hopeful thinking can be contagious. The impossible will start to feel possible when you spend more time hanging out with other hopeful ROCers living the above-the-line way.

Be hopeful. It suits you.

BE PRESENT (MANAWA)

The Hawaiian term for being present is manawa, which means bringing your attention to this moment in time. Not the moment before or the moment yet to come. The one you're in right now.

What are you doing right now? I'm staring at my computer screen as I write. What about you?

An easy way to remember manawa, another optimism boosting habit, is to remind yourself to be where your feet are. Look at your feet. That's where you are right now. Be there.

Bring your awareness and your thoughts back to your feet. Wriggle your toes, and notice whether they're touching your shoes. Are they hot or cold, wet or dry? Where are your feet planted on the planet right now? This will help you to not only calm your wandering mind, but also enjoy this moment in time.

Look at your feet. Be in that moment.

What can you see, hear, taste, feel and smell?

When you're present, you're not distracted and scattered, which means you're less likely to:

» make mistakes, because you are focussed and paying attention to 'now'

» forget information, because your brain has the space to hold it without needing to make room for unnecessary and distracting information

» be sidetracked, because you're in the zone

» lose concentration, which is a classic optimism blocker and powerful trigger for anxious thoughts and feelings.

At times you'll expect anxious thoughts to fly in because you're about to do something that will test your ROCability. It might be an exam, an interview for your first job, or stepping out of your comfort zone on school camp.

But they can also materialise quite unexpectedly. Anxious thoughts sideswipe you like a gale-force wind, stripping you of your power and dragging you down into the doom and gloom. Soon your anxious thoughts take over. You imagine the worst and your thoughts quickly slide below the line to trouble town. Has this happened to you?

Believe me when I tell you that no-one is immune to anxious thinking. Even the most popular, sporty, artsy, tall, short, smart, friendly, young, old, and even award-winning public speakers, singers and performers can get hooked by anxious below-the-line thinking.

Manawa is like getting a gentle hug whenever you feel anxious thoughts, feelings and emotions rising within you.

But then they look at their feet, and choose to be where they are. It brings them back to the present. Right here. Right now.

Manawa is like getting a gentle hug whenever you feel anxious thoughts, feelings and emotions rising within you. When they hook you in and hold you tight, **look at your feet and be where they are**. Don't rush yourself or get flustered. This isn't a race. Just be present so you can release the hook on your thoughts and soften the hold on your heart. Stay here, and stay for as long as you need.

TIPS FOR BEING PRESENT

Be where your feet are.

Engage your senses.

Keep eye contact.

Go at a slower pace.

Dedicate your thoughts and attention to whatever you're doing or whoever you're with.

BE QUIET (HAMAU)

Another reliable optimism booster is finding moments of quiet in your life (or as the local Hawaiians call it, hamau).

Our world is an orchestra of artificial sounds—people talking, music playing and devices beeping. From the moment you wake up you're surrounded by the sounds of life. Some soothing, some stress inducing.

Regular quiet times help you hit your 80:20 goal, especially when you're trying to keep your thoughts in perspective, maintain your buoyant mood and handle problems that come your way. Some noises can send you into a spin. Think of nails scraping on a blackboard, or the loud squeal of the assembly microphones being tested.

Ongoing exposure to artificial noise can make your brain feel overloaded and strained. Your brain doesn't do well in these situations, which may explain why you turn off the car stereo when you hear emergency sirens blazing. Reducing noise helps you to think more clearly and make better decisions.

Just like your body, your brain needs to rest and recharge so it can perform at its best. When your brain and nervous system get the chance to chill out, your body holds back on producing adrenaline and cortisol (the stress response chemicals). And that's got to be a good thing.

With so many bells and whistles competing for your attention, some people say silence is a dying phenomenon and so you need to work extra hard to find those quiet times.

Choosing quiet doesn't necessarily mean hiding away and cocooning yourself in meditation or ongoing isolation. *Hamau* is about separating yourself from noise from time to time so you can recharge.

If it's your thing, you can step off the grid and find quiet in nature. In Japan and Korea you can bathe in special forest areas filled only with nature and silence. But you don't need a designated area to plunge into nature. Home gardens, farm paddocks, nature trails and tracks are just as good.

If you have too much on your mind and you're doing everything on the fly, give *hamau* a try. You'll soon feel the benefits of adding quiet time to your self-care routine.

*Be aware that you
need to give yourself
regular quiet time.*

CHOOSE QUIET

» *Be aware that you need to give yourself regular quiet time.*

» *Turn distractions off and place devices on silent.*

» *Be in a space that promotes peace.*

» *Use noise-cancelling headphones if you have them.*

» *Get outside, sit on the sand, lay on your bed, ride your bike, or cuddle with your dog.*

» *Be silent, don't talk. Spend time with your thoughts.*

» *Listen for nature sounds—birds talking, rain falling, trees swaying in the wind or even your dog breathing.*

» *Silent moments are pockets of time filled with only naturally occurring noise provided by the chirping birds, crashing waves and swirling winds.*

Enjoy.

BE GRATEFUL (MAHALO)

Jayden was diagnosed with childhood arthritis. The condition causes extreme joint pain and swelling, and brought enormous stress and discomfort to his young body.

The pain in Jayden's body often stopped him doing things that he loved to do. Winter was the worst. The cold mornings made it difficult for his growing body to move freely, so he often arrived late for school.

My memory of this freezing cold morning was Jayden arriving around 10.30am looking quite uncomfortable. But as always he was grateful, (the Hawaiian word for which is *mahalo*). His mates were happy to see him, welcoming him with wrap-around hugs and high fives, and checking that he was doing okay.

Thinking back to that day, one moment stands out. I watched Jayden walk along on the verandah towards his friends, explaining why he was so late. They all listened intently, mesmerised as he spoke with an attitude of extreme gratitude despite his day starting so badly. He spent the morning immersed in a hot soothing bath, waiting for his pain medication to kick in. He knew he'd be late, and would need to catch up on school work. And he was missing out on time with his mates who were used to starting their day without him there (though they wished things were different).

In his own words, Jayden shared his belief that he had a choice. He could lie in the bath and sink in his own low, slow and heavy thinking. Or he could bring his attention back up and be grateful for the good in his life (of which there was plenty).

He acknowledged that he too had felt low many times before. And that was okay. (He was human, after all.) He didn't beat himself up. He simply gave himself permission to slip below the line.

Jayden's message stayed with me. Thoughts and emotions are like webs that are built and broken and built all over again. With his medical condition as his teacher, he learned the value of acknowledging (rather than ignoring) the stark reality of his personal situation and condition while choosing to focus on everything he could be grateful for. Over time he became aware that his thoughts could lift him up. And he preferred that feeling.

Jayden made *mahalo* his default, keeping his thoughts entwined in beautiful webs woven with thankfulness and gratitude. His friends, the activities he could do, hot baths, sleep-ins, caring people at school and his amazing dog were just some of the things he'd think about. The list was long. He designed it that way.

Be the aloha you want to
see in the world.

Jayden then shared a little more *mahalo* magic with the boys, telling them, "You need at least three grateful thoughts to combat one lacking thought." That tip worked well for him.

The world is full of bling, making it easy to get caught up wanting fancy things. You're led to believe you don't have enough, and need more to be happy. But *mahalo* has the power and grace to gently remind you of all the people, places and memories in your life, and how they all help you rise up to that awesome above-the-line space.

Now it's your turn to be grateful. Fill this space with anything and everything that's silky in your life.

Be the *aloha* you want to see in the world.

Be niele

Be manaolana

Be manawa

Be hanau

Be mahalo

YOUR ROC DREAM TEAM

As a teenager, you need a Dream Team that has your back more than ever. This is the ever-evolving mix of your family, friendship crew, mentors and even pets who will show up with bucketloads of unconditional love to teach, challenge and inspire you. That's a good thing.

If you've found your dream team, you're one of the lucky ones.

If you haven't found your dream team, and want to know how to find one, keep reading. All will be revealed.

Humans are born with an instinctive need to connect and hang out with other humans. It gives you the awesome feeling of belonging to something bigger than yourself.

When you make friends, join clubs and group chats, and play team sports, your sense of belonging increases. But there are no hard and fast rules here. It will look and feel different for everyone.

One thing you can be sure of is that being part of a good team of people can make you feel more complete. Humans don't like feeling alone or isolated. So much so that isolation is used as a form of punishment, which speaks volumes about the benefits of connecting with people.

Most people want to experience a Dream Team connection. And I'm sure you do too.

YOU ARE NOT ALONE

Have you ever felt disconnected, out of the loop or not part of a dream team? **You are not alone.**

Have you ever ducked or hidden away, but despite your best efforts couldn't stop yourself from falling below the line? **You are not alone.**

Have you ever put on a show and pretended you're all good? **You are not alone.**

Have you ever pretended your life is great, keeping up with other people's social media posts, pages and selfies that make their life look shiny and perfect? **You are not alone.**

Have you ever kept problems to yourself because you didn't want to bother anyone or create drama? **You are not alone.**

During times like these it's totally okay to channel your inner hermit crab. Scurry to your safe and snug-fitting shell where you can cry, feel sorry for yourself and sulk for a while. It's such

*Even when you're in
your shell, there will
be people who can help
and want to help.*

an above-the-line thing to do. Like all humans, you need to retreat and reset sometimes to take care of your mind, heart, body and soul. It's healthy, helpful, and a respectful way to care for yourself when you need to most.

But make sure you don't slide too far below the line. You can use your 'shell time' to boost yourself too.

Even when you're in your shell, there will be people who can help and want to help. They'll message, call, text and wave because they love you more than you could possibly know. But for them to gather around you, you need to let them in—not shut them out.

Let them love you to the moon and back.

But (there's always a 'but', and this one can't be sugar coated) no-one can ROC for you.

There are people who want to help you.

Let them in. They are your crew.

DREAM TEAM MEMBERS: YOUR CREW

Everyone has a crew. They're the people who get you, appreciate you, and respect you. They fit in with your weird and wonderful ways—even on your darkest and most sunny days. (Because let's be honest: we're all a bit weird and wonderful in one way or another.)

Your crew are the humans who add value to your life. And you add value to theirs, too.

Your crew should want you to succeed, and cheer the loudest when you do.

CALL IN YOUR CREW

Isn't it hilarious when adults say, "Just get some new friends" or "Hang out with different people at lunchtime if you're not happy"? Boy oh boy. If crew creation was that simple I wouldn't need to write this chapter because teenagers wouldn't feel lonely or disconnected—ever.

If you're interested in calling in your crew, either now or in years to come, here are seven steps that will make it easier for you.

STEP 1: CHECK IN

As always, I encourage you to check in with yourself and see where you're at right now. This gives you something to compare yourself with further along the track.

Write a few words that best describe how you feel right now. (It might be the very reason you want to call in your crew.)

_____

_____

_____

STEP 2: BE BRAVE (NOT FEARLESS)

You're ready to welcome people into your life. Acknowledging this takes bravery because you're admitting something is missing or you don't feel complete. Your bravery happens on the inside. It's subtle, but the people around you will notice and feel it.

STEP 3: BE CLEAR

Set your intentions. Being less wishy washy and more certain helps you to move closer to the right crew for you.

*Everyone has a crew.
They're the people who
get you, appreciate you,
and respect you.*

ANSWER THESE FIVE QUESTIONS:

1. Would you like to start calling in your crew?

_____

2. Why is this important to you?

_____

_____

_____

3. What qualities do you value in friendship?

_____

_____

_____

_____

4. What qualities do you have that you'd like to share with your crew?

_____

_____

_____

_____

5. How do you want to feel when you're around your crew?

_____

_____

_____

_____

_____

STEP 4: BE FLEXIBLE

Flexible behaviour is a key part of optimism. Sometimes you can get stuck in your old ways and keep doing the same thing, but for some weird reason expect to get a different result. That's okay. You're human. These things happen.

Now's the time to stretch and bend the habits you do every day. Maybe you go to the library at lunchtime every day of the week. Perhaps you've played soccer on the oval for the past four years, or keep missing out on chat time because you're usually late getting to school. Now's the time to mix it up a bit.

ANSWER THESE FOUR QUESTIONS:

1. Is there something you can change or do differently to make it easier for your crew to find you?

_____

_____

_____

_____

_____

2. Do you have a niggling fear that might be stopping you from calling in your crew?

_____

_____

_____

_____

_____

_____

_____

*Your kind of people
are out there. And
they're probably
looking for you too.*

3. If you do, then it's time to get friendly with fear. Can you switch your fear for freedom? (Not sure how? Check out page 145.)

_____

_____

_____

_____

4. Could a crew looking for you actually find you, or are you hidden out of sight?

_____

_____

_____

_____

STEP 5: BE A WORKER

My grandad used an old Scottish phrase: "Gie it laldy". Meaning 'give it everything you've got'. He always said this phrase when he wanted me to put as much gusto, effort and pride into what I was doing.

Calling in your crew is your chance to gie it laldy.

From little things big things grow.

STEP 6: BE PATIENT

It takes time to call people into your life who appreciate your humour, respect your fears and doubts, listen to your dreams, laugh with you and have your back, day or night.

Your crew may start with one person, grow to two, and then stretch to three, four or even more. But whatever the number, your kind of people are out there. And they're probably looking for you too.

So start calling them in. This isn't a sprint, but rather a steady jog that gives you the time and space to build the right friendship crew for you.

STEP 7: CHECK IN AGAIN

Remember to keep checking in. Look for the little signs and changes, because they're the optimism boosters you need to practise when you feel like giving up.

10 TIPS FOR FINDING THE RIGHT CREW FOR YOU

1. BE YOURSELF: *Being fake won't attract the right crew for you.*

2. SMILE: *It speaks volumes in any language. Let your face be the friendly, welcoming kind. Everyone loves to be smiled at.*

3. SAY "HI": *These two little letters form a brilliant little word that helps you connect and welcome people in.*

4. BECOME A LEGENDARY LISTENER: *If your voice isn't ready yet, and you're working on your bravery, let your ears do the work. Listen as if your life depends on it.*

5. ASK QUESTIONS: *Questions build connection and get conversations going. Be interested in people rather than trying to be interesting to people.*

6. BE PRESENT AND IN THE MOMENT: *Enjoy moments without the distraction of what went before or what's yet to come. Be where your feet are.*

7. LET THEM IN: *Be aware of other people trying to connect with you. Listen, look, and trust your intuition. Who is smiling, being present and questioning you?*

*Every day we make
decisions, change
plans, and tackle
challenges of various
shapes and sizes.*

8. CHANGE IT UP: *Say "Yes" to something new or different. Change your routine. Show up and get involved.*

9. REACH OUT: *Use social media to break the ice. Send a Happy Birthday message, make friendly comments, or say something nice.*

10. TRUST YOURSELF: *Back yourself and listen to your heart.*

You're on the right track. Keep going.
Just keep going.

FIND A MENTOR

Every day we make decisions, change plans, and tackle challenges of various shapes and sizes. And they can all make your life a bit hectic sometimes.

But that doesn't mean you have to deal with everything on your own.

Many young people are getting extra support from a mentor—someone (usually older) who is outside their friendship group, but inside their circle of trusted people.

Of course, like every other ROC suggestion in this book, it's your decision whether or not to invite a mentor into your life. If it feels right, go for it. If it doesn't, then that's okay too.

It's also a great idea to run it past your parents.

Mentors are coaches, family friends, group leaders or club members. They don't take sides. Instead, they listen and talk things through.

Think of the movies you've seen where characters in the story become mentors to other characters (the mentees).

Movies are filled with mentor-mentee relationships. And they're easy to spot once you know what you're looking for. Professor Dumbledore shared wisdom and life lessons with Harry Potter. Watch the Lion King and you'll notice Mufasa teaching and inspiring his son Simba. And in Star Wars, Obi-Wan Kenobi offered endless advice and direction to Luke Skywalker.

Like those in the movies, your mentor could be the person helping you to bounce back, keep your eye on your goals, and stay above the line.

Mentoring someone is an enormous privilege. The person you choose will feel both proud and incredibly honoured when you ask them. And don't forget to look beyond the obvious when reaching out. I know young people who are being mentored by teachers, neighbours, grandparents and sporting coaches, to name a few.

You'll know when the time is right to ask a trusted person in your life to be your mentor. You don't have to rush it. The universe has a funny way of providing the things you need when you need them.

Does this idea appeal to you?

Do you have someone in mind? (If you do, you should probably check in with your parents first.)

NOT ENOUGH OR TOO MUCH

It's important to remember that you are the way you are for a reason.

All your quirks and your craziness on windy days make you ... well, you. Sometimes that won't be enough for others, and at other times it will be way too much.

It can be hard work trying to please everyone, especially when there are probably several hundred people in your year at school and billions of people on the planet. If you wanted to be a perfect match for all these people, where would you start? And where would you stop?

*The right people will show
up and shine for you.
They'll find a way to stay
in your life.*

Forget about chasing people, groups of people, or those seemingly perfect 'got my entire life together' kind of people. You don't need to fight for a spot, or exhaust yourself trying to be someone you're not.

The right people will show up and shine for you. They'll find a way to stay in your life, and you'll find a way to stay in theirs.

Be with humans who see your magic.
Go where you're loved and recognised,
not where you're ruined and criticised.

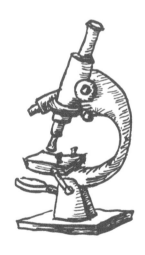

ROC BOOSTER: PERMISSION TO BE YOU

Maybe you've been described as too loud, too chatty or too 'in your face'. Or perhaps you've heard on the grapevine that you're too quiet, too shy, and you play the game of life too slowly.

Never assume that loud is right or wrong.

Never assume that being strong, confident, quiet or shy is good or bad.

The voices and opinions of others can be incredibly strong and convincing. So here's your chance to lay your cards on the table and write down all the ways you've overheard or been told you're too much or not enough.

_____

_____

_____

_____

_____

Be loud, be quiet, be sensitive, be strong. Be whatever you are and do it well.

Perhaps your 'too much' was passed down through the generations of your family. It could be a gift from your mum, your dad or your grandparents. That's the miracle of DNA (genetic memory passed from generation to generation). Wear your 'too much' DNA with pride. It's the gift that keeps on giving.

There might be a good reason for you being 'too much' or 'not enough'. It may become your strength and your gift to the world in your future career. It may be just what someone is looking for in a life partner. Or it may be the characteristic needed for someone to explore the world and make it a better place.

What if your 'too much' or 'not enough' is your unique point of difference but you just don't know it yet?

GIVE YOURSELF PERMISSION TO BE:

cranky, interesting, caring, arty, scared, gentle, rough, tough, loud, gross, masculine, feminine, smart, fast, boring, wrong, funny, sensitive, bold, friendly, rude, loving, generous, sleepy, stingy, dreamy, curious, adventurous, shy, frustrated, honest, annoyed, kind, sneaky, creative, lonely, thoughtful, weak, fearful, confused, in love, confident, right, exhausted, selfish, tough, serious, jealous, quiet, strong, sad, weird, happy, and above all YOU.

*There's no
one-size-fits-all
solution to forming
friendships and
relationships.*

LOOK, LIFT, LEAVE

When my son was little I'd remind him of my three play rules: friendly, safe and fair (FSF). I'm sure these popped into his mind whenever he played with his friends to keep the games and friendships flowing.

Fast forward to the teenage years, and FSF has been replaced with LLL: **LOOK, LIFT OR LEAVE.**

When I share this idea with teenagers they love it. Why? Because it's real, it's doable, and it removes fakeness (something I know you can sense better than a sniffer dog at the airport).

I understand you want to be yourself, fit in, and be with your crew. But you're not going to approve of, like or agree with everyone you meet. And not everyone will approve of, like or agree with you at school, at parties, or on your sporting team.

With this in mind, there's no one-size-fits-all solution to forming friendships and relationships. But the three L's embrace a simple rule: show kindness and respect.

Let me explain.

> **LOOK** – Be on the lookout for the talents, strengths and positive points of difference in other people. Look for the kindness, humour,

honesty and compassion they bring to your group, class or team. When you're looking for the good, you're helping them to ROC inside.

LIFT – Get creative and find ways you can actively lift other people up with your thoughts, words, actions and interactions—both in person and online. Give compliments, smile, encourage, acknowledge their goodness, and show your appreciation towards them. Again, when you're lifting you're helping them rise above the line.

LEAVE – Don't hassle, hurt, annoy, put down, embarrass or exclude anyone or make their life difficult in person or online. Don't be the human obstacle that stops them ROCing and rising.

When your group of friends has five, ten or 15 people in it, there's a chance that one of them might not float your boat. If that's the case you can choose to look, lift or leave them alone. Leaving doesn't mean you have to leave the group or the party. You're simply making the ROC decision to leave them be and stay out of their way. Let others ROC and rise and you will too.

Humans follow humans. That's what we do. But here's a powerful tip I read many years ago: gossip runs out of energy when it hits a ROCer's heart and ears. Why? Because when you ROC, you choose to block gossip from spreading its ugliness any further. You make the above-the-line choice not to be part of the problem, but rather to be part of the ROC and rise revolution.

There's power in knowledge, and there's weight in numbers.

Looking, Lifting, and Leaving is your responsibility.

BE A ROC CHAMPION

ROC champions are ordinary people that show up for people they care about. You can be a ROC champion for your crew. And your friends and family can also be a ROC champion for you.

Someone in your friendship group or extended family may be feeling stuck or in a funk. It may be the last person you'd expect because a person's external behaviour rarely matches what's going on in their mind, heart and body. (As the saying goes, "You can't judge a book by its cover".)

It can be hard to know what to do when a friend is feeling flat and finding it hard to ROC. Do you ask them if everything is okay? Do you send them a message? Do you invite them over? Or do you keep your distance?

Being a ROC champion doesn't mean you need to fix or solve everything. That's not your job—or your responsibility.

*Being a ROC
champion doesn't
mean you need to fix
or solve everything.*

All you can do is trust yourself and do what you feel is right. There's no right or wrong way to show up, smile, be kind, care and listen.

If you're an empath (someone who is sensitive and regularly takes on the worries and feelings of others as if they were their own), be extra careful and use lots of boosters to care for your own mental and emotional fitness. After helping a friend who's in a funk I make sure I do the Harry Shake, take soothing ROC breaths, and listen to great music. This helps me to be a ROC champion without losing myself along the way.

ROC champions look for changes in both their own and their friends':

» attitude and energy. (Does something feel different or not quite right?)

» thoughts, conversations, heart talk and body talk. (Are they slipping below the line?)

» exercise and movement routines

» sleeping and eating patterns

» socialising and involvement in group chats or social media

Chances are you're in someone else's Dream Team, which means they think you're reliable and trustworthy just the way you are. You need only to show up, care and be there. No need to be a superhero. Being a ROC champion is enough.

If your gut is telling you that your friend needs more than you can give, please listen to it. (That's your intuition stepping in to give you a helping hand.) Talk to an adult, a teacher, your mentor or a person in your own Dream Team so they can help your friend too.

You don't need to fly solo, even if your friend has asked you not to tell anyone.

Trust your gut.

Listen to your intuition.

Be a ROC champion—an ordinary person who shows up and cares.

ROCING ON SOCIAL MEDIA

I don't want to go too deep into the challenges and perils of social media. You've probably heard experts who specialise in this topic speak at your school, and I recommend asking them for advice.

But I couldn't write a book for teenagers without at least touching on this topic. It's part of your life. And it looks like it's here to stay.

Social media is evolving at an incredible pace, giving the chance to communicate 24/7. But many of the platforms and interactions are a raging fire burning out of control, fuelled by comments and conversations that could potentially block you from ROCing and rising.

While you can't control the actions and choices of the other users, there are some things you can control. You can control your thoughts, heart talk and body talk, as well as how you engage with, react to and respond to what appears on your screen.

Let's keep it simple.

When you're active on social media, you've got to be ROC solid. Social media can be brutal and cruel, and users can be incredibly mean-spirited at times. But it sucks you in, and before you know it you're trapped inside the danger zone of doubt, worry and uncertainty.

You can control your involvement on social media by asking yourself two questions.

When you log in, you're choosing to step into the land of posts, tags, comments, likes, emojis, photos, group chats and messages. Some are ROC boosters, while others are ROC blockers.

I understand how the fear of missing out (FOMO) can pull you in, take over and keep you in the zone. But what if the fear of falling (FOF) below the line was stronger than FOMO? Imagine if FOF thoughts helped you decide to leave a group, disengage from a conversation, or choose not to share, view or comment. This simple choice could lead you to a happier, above-the-line place. It's worth thinking about.

ENTER AT YOUR OWN RISK

You can't control the action of others on social media. But you can control your involvement on social media by asking yourself two questions.

Before you comment, share, like, engage or post a photograph or video, ask yourself:

> » Will this help others to ROC and rise?
> » Will this help me to ROC and rise?

If you answer "No" to either question then stop what you're doing and step away from your device. Nothing good will come from it.

Remember the Look, Lift or Leave rules? They will help you to leave a stamp on social media that's above the line rather than below. And in doing so you'll join the millions of teenagers who answered "Yes". It's not too late to make the switch. It's never too late.

If your answer is YES, then good on you.

"Yes" is above the line in so many ways. Teenagers around the world are thanking you right now. Seriously, answering "Yes" might not feel like a big deal. But if millions of teenagers say "Yes", that collective choice has the power to create an enormous wave of change.

If you feel like your ROC armour is constantly being cracked, bruised and battered, social media may not be the best place for you right now. If it's blocking you from rising, consider taking a break so you can keep on boosting, believing and building yourself up from the inside out.

> *Log on with good intentions.*
> *Be ROC solid when you're online.*
> *If all you see, read, hear or feel is*
> *blocking you from ROCing,*
> *leave so you can ROC and rise.*

OPTIMISM BOOSTERS

Over the years, thousands of teenagers have asked me how to keep their optimism levels topped up. I like the fact you want to take charge of this, which is why I've included simple optimism boosters.

I suggest using these boosters *before* you desperately need them. Why? Because the sooner you realise you're falling (by noticing your thoughts, heart talk and body talk), the sooner you can stop yourself from falling and lift yourself up.

....
OPTIMISM BOOSTER: HYGGE HAVEN
....

Following the arrows painted on the IKEA floor, three teenage girls caught my eye. I could hear them talking about their bedroom, and how they wanted it to be cosy so they could chill out and relax. They were mixing and matching the perfect blend of cushions, candles and throw rugs.

I had a hunch the girls had heard of *hygge* (pronounced 'hoo gah'), a Norwegian word that means 'to create a cosy, safe place and space of your own'. *Hygge* is a long-valued way of thinking and living in Denmark.

*Being in your haven
helps you lower your
stress and calm your
nervous system.*

In my home I call it my haven. It's quiet, familiar and comfy—perfect for resting my head, heart and body.

Creating a haven in your home, indoors or out, is a great way to start a self-care routine. Being in your haven helps you lower your stress, stop those anxious thinking patterns, and calm your nervous system if it's racing out of control. *Hygge* is choosing love, connecting, and enjoying time to chill in your special haven space.

One of the main ideas behind *hygge* is to leave technology at the door—not because it's a bad thing, but because you can then feel the value of removing all distractions and giving your full attention to this moment.

When I think back to the girls I saw in IKEA, I wonder if they were indeed gathering bits and pieces for their *hygge* haven.

When you retreat to your self-made haven, you're well placed to boost your mental fitness, chill out, and be with yourself. You can also choose to be with people near and dear to you. This will increase your sense of belonging and happiness, and your body will release its happy chemicals so you feel good on the inside.

Do you have a haven you can retreat to?

Would you like to create one?

Your haven doesn't need to be fancy or costly. You can create it by rearranging bits and pieces you already own, or fossicking around for the perfect addition at a charity shop. Your *hygge* haven could be a comfy chair and a throw rug, or even your favourite spot on the couch. As long as it's safe, comfy, and you like being there, you're on to a winner.

HAVEN BENEFITS

Hygge time is free. You just need to create it.

There is no right or wrong.

Fill your haven with talking, laughing and storytelling, friends and food, or make it a peaceful time with yourself wrapped in a cosy blanket with music and movies.

Incorporating haven time into your life will boost your body's feel-good chemical production, which will lift you above the line.

OPTIMISM BOOSTER: MUSIC MATTERS

Music has the power to bring people together, connect cultures, and bridge language barriers. It can also be a boosting element of your self-care routine, especially when you're trying to change your thoughts or your mood.

Your taste in music is as personal as your taste in food, so the way you choose and use music to support your mental fitness is totally up to you too.

Whether you're listening to music, creating it, drumming to it or humming along with it, select music that's in tune with your emotions. What you listen to can affect the way you react to people, how you respond to STUFF, and even the choices you make.

Music is a reliable ROC booster. It can fire you up and calm you down as it cleverly engages the parts of the brain that are in charge of your emotions, attention and memory.

There are so many links between music and mental fitness. Some say it can even trigger the release of dopamine—a savvy brain chemical that assists you to feel more motivated and energised.

You've probably got endless playlists. But do any of those playlists target your mood? The best time to create your

*Your personal playlists
can reduce anxious
feelings, soothe stress
levels, and inspire you to
think differently.*

mood making playlists is when you're feeling pretty good rather than when you're feeling low, lonely or cranky.

Given the chance, your personal playlists can reduce anxious feelings, soothe stress levels, and inspire you to think differently.

Get busy creating playlists that:

» encourage you to be up

» keep you up when you're feeling fab

» relax and calm you

» lift your mood if you're feeling a bit flat or down

» energise you

» fire you up so you can get the things on your 'to do' list done

» boost your optimism if it has taken a hit

We can't talk about music without mentioning singing. Singing can release other savvy feel-good chemicals such as endorphins and oxytocin, which are natural anxiety and stress busters. Sing in the shower, your bedroom or the car. No-one cares how good or bad you are. (And if they do, it's none of their business.) Just keep singing. It's good for you.

Music can also drag you down. Some music can even hold you in a pattern of repetitive below-the-line thinking. So be smart, and notice how you feel when listening to particular music. If it's dragging you down, press STOP and make a new selection.

Does your music lift you up? Does it pull you down? What song lyrics inspire you?

_____

_____

_____

_____

_____

Does some music remind you of good times, great people and amazing experiences?

Consider adding these songs to your playlists.

We all have a go-to song. One that means something to us, with lyrics and a vibe that have a profound effect on the way we feel. That's your ROC song.

What's your ROC song?

_____

Now is a great time to get busy and create a few new playlists. Some playlist ideas include:

- » lift me up
- » keep me up
- » celebrate
- » chill
- » kindness and self-care

Let music be your buddy
so its rhythm lifts you up.
Let its lyrics charge your heart
and its words soothe your mood.
Let your music bring you
all the wild courage and
confidence you need.
ROC and rise.
Press play and repeat.

*Animals can calm and
reassure you if you're
feeling worried, anxious
or fearful.*

OPTIMISM BOOSTER: THE POWER OF FUR FRIENDS

Could an animal be part of your Dream Team, or even join you in your *hygge* haven?

Animals such as dogs and cats are here for a relatively short time compared to humans. But they sure do cram a lot into their lives. With pinpoint precision they can wriggle their way into your life and heart, building memories and leaving pawprints that are powerful and profound.

I've always known how much animals can calm and reassure us if we're feeling worried, anxious or fearful. My dog Harry is proof of that. But so is Kyzer, a four-year-old Golden Retriever. He's a therapy dog who works in schools and places with teenagers. And he took my understanding of animal magic to a whole new level.

Kyzer was working at a school where I was giving a presentation. I was told he liked to lounge around with the kids in the library at lunchtime, and so I made it my business to be there too. As expected, Kyzer was Mr Popular, with students huddled all around him. It was a love fest, and Kyzer was winning.

Taking a moment to be where my feet were, I stood back and took in the view. It was glaringly obvious that every teenager in his zone was smiling, calm and content as they gently stroked his face, back and super-soft ears. They were drinking in his love and kindness.

It was quite mesmerising.

I watched as he turned to face students—precious moments as they stopped and looked directly into his big brown eyes. They chatted and gently whispered to him in the most beautiful way.

Teens were talking and Kyzer was listening.

Kyzer had mastered the art of doing one thing at a time, and he was encouraging each student to do the same. Thoughts of homework, tests, friends and after-school routines disappeared from their minds, as if suspended in time. They were all caught in Kyzer's magic spell.

Like many dogs, Kyzer was born with all the tools needed to remind us to slow down, do one thing at a time, and love unconditionally. Most animals can remind us to do these things, which makes them great for our mental fitness.

If you have a pet in your home, you're lucky. They don't judge or criticise because they're too busy loving you all the way to the moon and back. If it seems like you're sliding below the line, your pet could be just what you need to restore balance in your mind, heart, body and soul.

DID YOU KNOW THAT BEING WITH AN ANIMAL CAN HELP ...

» *reduce feelings of loneliness*

» *boost your mood*

» *keep problems in perspective*

» *slow your heart rate*

» *lower your blood pressure*

» *keep you active and outdoors*

» *keep you calm or lift you up*

» *decrease stress hormones*

» *increase soothe hormones*

» *hug your heart*

*Clutter crowds both
your physical space
and your ROC
thinking space.*

OPTIMISM BOOSTER: CLEAR CLUTTER

When I first met Abby, she felt unorganised and totally overwhelmed. She'd fallen into the clutter trap, constantly chasing her tail and rushing from A to B.

Abby's personal space was in turmoil. Her books and notes were scattered everywhere, her clothes were piled high, and her bedroom floor was a place of mess and wild confusion.

She regularly found herself rushing and panicking, grabbing things she needed at the last minute as she ran out the door. She was drowning in her own clutter.

Her thoughts were also in turmoil as she raced against the clock, desperately trying to meet deadlines, submit assignments and turn up on time.

Something had to change.

Here's the thing: clutter crowds both your physical space and your ROC thinking space.

Abby needed help with both. But most of all she needed to get rid of the clutter because less clutter leads to clearer and calmer thinking.

If this sounds familiar, call for a clear out so you can organise and manage your space. When you know where all your stuff is, your mind doesn't have to work so hard. And let's face it: you've got enough to think about already.

Abby needed a plan. And so might you, so here's what I suggest you do.

> » Slow the flow of stuff entering your space (to stop anything adding to the clutter).
> » Sort out the easy clutter first (just as you'd start with the easier questions on a test).

For each item, ask yourself whether you'll:

> » keep it
> » recycle it
> » pay it forward
> » donate it
> » sell it
> » store it
> » bin it

Clearing clutter takes time, and it can be tiring (not to mention boring). So sort one space at a time, whether it's a drawer, your school bag or a shelf in your wardrobe. You could even invite a friend to do it with you.

But don't stop there. Technology can also lead to messy and cluttered thinking.

DO A TECH SORT TOO

» Delete, save and sort folders on your devices.

» Delete apps you no longer use.

» Sort through messages, private groups and photos.

» Store or recycle old devices, cables and chargers.

Every time you clear clutter, you're giving yourself the chance to think without unnecessary stress. That's a good habit to get into.

It took Abby a few weeks to clear her clutter. But she agreed the time was well spent. When it was done she felt more organised, sorted, and in control.

Give it a go.
Clear the clutter,
one space at a time.

A vision and vibe board is a ROC booster you can add to any time you like.

Choose five spaces that are calling out to be cleared.

1. _____

2. _____

3. _____

4. _____

5. _____

OPTIMISM BOOSTER: VISION AND VIBE BOARD

The only rule to keep in mind when creating your vision and vibe (V&V) board is to remember it's not just something you do at the beginning of the year. It's a ROC booster you can add to any time you like.

I'm a mega-fan of V&V boards. They're a great way to:

» get clear on what matters to you—family, friends, health, your dog or your team

» bring more above-the-line quotes, colours, words and pictures into your life

» keep you on track if you're working towards a goal or dream

» visualise the things you want more of—friendship, fitness, a holiday with your family, or perhaps money for your first car

» power up your altar. (I'll be talking about this in the next section.)

» start your day—use it to raise your vibe in the morning. Spend a moment gazing at your board, drinking in all the positive energy immersed within it

» end your day—before you go to bed, repeat what you did in the morning. This will help you drift off to sleep rather than replaying the day's events over and over in your mind

MAKE YOUR VISION AND VIBES COME ALIVE

1. Get a photo of you that you love. One that radiates your personality, happiness, pride, confidence, or that has an awesome memory attached to it.

2. Gather up scissors, glue, magazines, Instagram images, quotes and any other bits and pieces you love. (Think 'crafty' and 'recycled'. And remember, there are no rules.)

3. Give yourself as much time as you need. It should be a project of love, not a dash to the finish line. Play

your favourite playlist, eat mood-boosting food, and be with friends or by yourself.

4. Be a daydream believer. If an idea pops into your mind, you might not understand it yet. But chances are it has popped up for a reason, so add it to your V&V board.

5. Don't be swayed by trends. Allow yourself to be led by your own head and heart, because that's when your vision and vibe does its best work.

6. Leave space for new ideas, and check in often to see whether you're feeling the vibe you deserve.

The Optimism Recap — Section 3

I'm so happy for you, because you now have the tools and boosters you need to be optimistic and spend more time on the bright side of life. You can't buy or borrow optimism, but you can always practise it.

You now have 16 optimism boosters at your disposal.

If you choose one booster a day, you'll be living more of the 80:20 way in just 16 days. So now's the time to practise your strengths and work on your weaknesses. It's the ROC way.

Be the shining optimist in your life. Ready, set, go.

16 WAYS IN 16 DAYS

1. **Add 'yet'** – Use this ROC wish word to keep your hopeful thoughts strong.

2. **Be curious** – Ask questions and be open minded at every opportunity.

3. **Be hopeful** – Your attitude and thoughts are expecting good things to happen.

4. **Be present** – Be where your feet are.

5. **Be quiet** – Take time to enjoy moments of peace and quiet. Let your nervous system rest.

6. **Be grateful** – Train your brain to focus on what's working well and the abundance in your life.

7. **Call in your crew** – Make sure you're surrounded by people who are right for you.

8. **Think about getting a mentor** – Is there a person who comes to mind?

9. **Enough** – Too much? You're great just the way you are. Be you.

10. **LOOK, LIFT, LEAVE** – We all have a responsibility to help others ROC and rise too.

11. **Be a ROC champion** – Be an ordinary person who shows up and cares.

12. *Hygge* **haven** – Create a space where you can totally relax when you need it the most.

13. **Your music matters** – Choose tunes that boost and soothe.

14. **Fur friends** – You will never feel lonely when your fur friends are around.

15. **Clear clutter** – Less clutter creates more space for ROC thinking.

16. **Vision and vibe board** – Let your wildest dreams and wishes come alive.

Notes & ROC Reminders

Take some time to reflect on what you've read in
Section 3 about optimism. What caught your eye? What
thoughts and ideas were triggered? What do you want
to make sure you don't forget?

_____

_____

_____

_____

_____

_____

_____

_____

_____

_____

_____

_____

SECTION 4

CRUISING WITH CONFIDENCE

CRUISING WITH CONFIDENCE

Being confident feels good inside. But everyone experiences confidence in their own way. There's no right or wrong way to feel confident.

However, there is a common trend that leads the way.

You now know the collective power of your thoughts. So it makes sense to choose thoughts that remind you that you are capable, can trust yourself, and have got what it takes to show up with courage and bravery. (That doesn't mean fear, worry or doubt aren't there. It just means you're tipping the balance in your favour.)

Whether your personality is loud and 'out there', or quiet and less 'out there' is irrelevant. Thinking and talking to yourself with confidence is an inside job. And you don't need a microphone, audience or funny joke to do it. You can quietly have robust and confident thoughts that inspire you to join the team, start a conversation, or share your opinion in a class discussion.

As I mentioned earlier, you can't judge a book by its cover. And judging someone's confidence by their appearance or actions is fraught with danger. Some of the most confident, sure and solid teenagers I know are quiet, while others are quite loud. But they all have what it takes to think confidently and show it in a way that's right for them.

Your confident thoughts, heart talk and body talk all have consequences. You boost your mental fitness and elevate yourself above the line, living the 80:20 way.

This section is filled with rituals and boosters. Practise them often to help you grow your confidence, inside and out.

CONFIDENCE IS	CONFIDENCE IS NOT
✓ Trusting yourself	✗ Being better than anyone else
✓ Being sure of your abilities	✗ Always being loud and out there
✓ Quietly knowing you're capable	✗ Telling everyone how good you are
✓ Thinking 'I can'	✗ Seeing others as your competition
✓ Relying on your own skills	✗ Instant and immediate
✓ Being ready to have a go	✗ Popularity
✓ Believing in yourself	✗ Easy for everyone
✓ Taking risks without needing a particular result	✗ A permanent feeling
✓ Learning from failures	✗ Only for extroverts
✓ Being yourself	✗ The same for everyone
✓ Knowing your strengths and weaknesses	✗ Following others
✓ Thinking above-the-line thoughts	✗ Set and forget

---

*Changing STUFF
keeps you on your toes
and up to date. But it
can also make you feel
that life's a race.*

THE BIG SIX

Right now, your life may be a complex mix of brilliance and total confusion. And it can test your confidence in a big way.

You've hit an age milestone (your teens) where you start developing your own opinions, attitudes and beliefs about yourself and the world. And unless you've been living in a cave, you've probably noticed that the stuff in your life can change as quickly as you do.

Changing STUFF keeps you on your toes and up to date. But it can also make you feel that life's a race, and you're holding on with all your might. With this in mind, it makes sense that teenagers are so keen to talk about six big questions (which I call the Big Six).

(Most teenagers talk to me privately about these questions after I've presented at their school or in a coaching session. My guess is they think they're the only person who's asking them. But that's so not true. Millions of teenagers are wondering about the Big Six. So you can breathe a sigh of relief and just read on.)

THE BIG SIX QUESTIONS ARE:

1. Who am I?

2. Where do I fit in?

3. Who am I important to?

4. What's important to me?

5. What am I good at?

6. What's my purpose?

If you find yourself asking these questions, it's an above-the-line sign you're trying to find your place in the world. And that's what you're supposed to do in your teenage years.

But there's a catch. Asking these questions can make you feel a little unsettled, unsure, doubtful and uncertain. You're no longer a child but still not quite an adult, which can make this a crazy age and stage in your life. You never asked yourself these questions when you were in Year Three. But now they keep popping up at the most annoying times, such as when you're trying to fall asleep or you're alone and feeling out of the loop.

This is normal (whatever that is).

When you ask the Big Six, you're exploring. You're finding out where you fit, how you're valued, and discovering all the greatness you can offer the world.

Again, this is normal.

Sometimes you know.

It takes bravery to ask the Big Six. Like giving yourself a big boosting hug, you'll feel certain, safe and secure when you know the answers. It's normal to have unstoppable days when you can answer each question confidently. You nail it, and your mind, heart and body tell you so.

Sometimes you don't know.

But what about when you don't have an answer? You keep looking, but the answers are nowhere to be found. You feel yourself slipping below the line, and start doubting yourself in a big way.

You may also become the expert at finding friends and acquaintances who are nailing it (apparently), which drags you even further below the line.

This is when you need next-level bravery.

*You keep chopping
and changing, trying to
work out what you like
and dislike.*

HERE'S HOW EASILY AND QUICKLY THE BIG SIX QUESTIONS CAN SHOW UP:

1. YOUR TASTE in music, movies, people and fashion is changing. And it's so different from everyone else's. You keep chopping and changing, trying to work out what you like and dislike. It feels like you're trying to keep up with yourself, which is hard work (and confusing).

You ask yourself, "Who am I?"

2. YOU'RE TRYING to make the move from one friendship group to another. You're in limbo—not quite out, but not quite in either. You want to feel like you belong, and that someone has your back. But it's taking so long, and you're wondering if you've made the right decision. Panic sets in.

You ask yourself, "Where do I fit in?"

3. YOU HAVEN'T BEEN included in a newly created group chat (or you sense you've been added only as an afterthought). Your overthinking mind turns up to shine, and you're wondering and pondering below the line.

You ask yourself, "Who am I important to?"

4. YOU WATCH the news, YouTube and Instagram. You see posts and threads with images that catch your eye. You look for like-minded people as you read up on important issues and want to discuss topics that spark your heart and tick your boxes.

You ask yourself, "What's important to me?"

5. YOU'VE JOINED groups, tried new things, and looked high and low for a hobby or sport that floats your boat. You've signed up and dropped out so many times that you're ready to give up. To top it off, you weren't selected for the team you dreamed of being in. But you love it, and you're good at it. It feels so cruel and unfair.

You ask yourself, "What am I good at?"

6. YOU DON'T KNOW what you'll do when you leave school, and you have absolutely no ideas (yet). You see others making decisions as if their life is perfectly planned. You search and dig, wondering what gifts you have to offer the planet. It's frustrating, and drags your thoughts below the line.

You ask yourself, "What's my purpose?"

To ask the Big Six is brave. But to beat yourself up for not knowing the answers is a supreme ROC blocker. It will trap you in a world of worry, fear, doubt and anxious thinking. Yuck.

HERE'S HOW TO TURN IT AROUND

1. YOUR TASTE in music, movies, people and fashion is changing. And it's so different from everyone else's. You keep chopping and changing, trying to work out what you like and dislike. It feels like you're trying to keep up with yourself, which is hard work (and confusing).

You ask yourself, "Who am I?"

You reply, "I'm finding out what I like. Life is a smorgasbord of music, movies and fashion waiting for me to try, and the answers will come in good time. There's no deadline, just chance after chance to shine in my ROC light."

You want to feel like you belong, and that someone has your back.

2. YOU'RE TRYING to make the move from one friendship group to another. You're in limbo—not quite out, but not quite in either. You want to feel like you belong, and that someone has your back. But it's taking so long, and you're wondering if you've made the right decision. Panic sets in.

You ask yourself, "Where do I fit in?"

You reply, "I'm switching groups for a reason, so I'll keep going. It's normal to feel lost in the middle, but soon I'll be settled and feel like I fit in. I just need to be patient and press on. It will be worth it."

3. YOU HAVEN'T BEEN included in a newly created group chat (or you sense you've been added only as an afterthought). Your overthinking mind turns up to shine, and you're wondering and pondering below the line.

You ask yourself, "Who am I important to?"

You reply, "I know I'm important to _____, _____ and _____. This feeling will fade as I keep calling in my crew, who will welcome me in with all their heart. When I do, I'll look back on this and be so happy I chose to push through."

4. YOU WATCH the news, YouTube and Instagram. You see posts and threads with images that catch your eye. You look for like-minded people as you read up on important issues and want to discuss topics that spark your heart and tick your boxes.

You ask yourself, "What's important to me?"

You reply, "I'm curious, and I'm finding out what ignites my interest. I'll keep exploring and learning, and as I do those like-minded people will show up and shine. Until then I can keep following what's important to me, even if it isn't set in concrete yet."

5. YOU'VE JOINED groups, tried new things, and looked high and low for a hobby or sport that floats your boat. You've signed up and dropped out so many times that you're ready to give up. To top it off, you weren't selected for the team you dreamed of being in. But you love it, and you're good at it. It feels so cruel and unfair.

You ask yourself, "What am I good at?"

You reply, "I have plenty of time to work it out. In the meantime I'll stick with it, say yes to opportunities and challenges, and keep an open mind."

6. YOU DON'T KNOW what you'll do when you leave school, and you have absolutely no ideas (yet). You see others making decisions as if their life is perfectly planned. You search and dig, wondering what gifts you have to offer the planet. It's frustrating, and drags your thoughts below the line.

You ask yourself, "What's my purpose?"

You reply, "I wonder when my precious gifts and talents will be unwrapped and revealed to the world. I have places to go, people to meet and adventures to seek."

Beating yourself up
when the answers
don't magically appear
in front of you is a
supreme ROC blocker.

As I said, to ask the Big Six is brave. And to have no clear answer is a natural part of the human journey, no matter how old you are. Do yourself a favour, and ask your mum, dad, aunty or coach whether they know the answers to the Big Six every day of the week. Do they? Or does it fluctuate? Some days they can probably nail it. But on other days they may not even be able to find the nails.

Beating yourself up when the answers don't magically appear in front of you is a supreme ROC blocker. Don't do it.

ROC RITUALS

Spring arrives, and Australians are swooped again and again as 'magpie season' begins.

This territorial bird doesn't care how old you are, how tall you are, or how fast you're riding your bike. The magpie is in 'protect my babies' mode, and without warning it will manoeuvre through the air to dive-bomb you with pinpoint accuracy.

Like most people I had one area I always had to carefully navigate during magpie season. (For me it was a section of a nearby park.) I couldn't go around it. I had to go through it.

So I made a survive-the-swoop plan:

» Wear a brimmed hat, keep my eyes down and scream wildly.

» Wave a massive stick (my armour of choice) above my head.

» Run as fast as I could through the gum trees, which were chock-a-block with magpies.

I ran that gauntlet for five consecutive magpie seasons. And thanks to my trusty survive-the-swoop plan I usually got through unscathed. Without it, I would have been struck and wounded for sure.

I'm a big believer in having a plan and using daily rituals to survive life's swooping moments.

ROC rituals are about caring for yourself, digging deep, and using your boosters to stay above the line when you know you'll be up against it and can feel a subtle swoop coming your way.

ROC rituals are especially handy when you know you'll be:

» going into tough territory

» in the company of people who haven't yet mastered the art of LOOKING for the good, LIFTING others up and LEAVING people alone.

Just as I used my plan to help me survive the magpie season, you can use ROC rituals to help you get ready for school, plan for a party, head to your next class, engage on social media, wait in the canteen line at recess or step on the bus at the end of the day.

Until the entire world knows how to LOOK, LIFT and LEAVE, try these gentle rituals. They'll help you survive the swoop and keep thriving.

ROC RITUAL TRIO

I recommend three simple rituals to lift your self-care routine.

» go to your altar

» be wrapped

» get grounded

GO TO YOUR ALTAR

Altars have been around for centuries—in churches, mosques, temples, homes and gardens all around the world.

As a young person in a rapidly changing world, you need a sacred space that reminds you of your worth and importance more than ever.

Your ROC altar can lift your mood by reminding you of everything that's important to you.

An altar is a simple ROC tool that boosts you up and reassures you when you're feeling flat or below the line. They're also awesome to use when you're above the line and want to stay there.

Altars don't have to be a big deal. And it's totally up to you whether you create one for yourself. If you do, keep it simple and remember it can be as small as a napkin or as large as a shelf on your bookcase. Your altar, your choice.

HOW TO CREATE A ROC ALTAR

What you place on your altar is totally up to you. But your V&V board could be a great place to start. My altar has precious pictures, hearts, shells, cards, and even a beautiful amethyst brooch that belonged to my Gran. And they all have special meaning to me. When I spend time enjoying my altar (usually a few minutes each day), I get a hit of happiness straight to my heart. It's free, it feels good, and I like it.

Your ROC altar can:

> » Lift your mood by reminding you of everything that's important to you.

> » Bring your focus back to the present moment so you can think more optimistically.

» Remind you of your worth, and that no-one has the right to dent it.

Showing up at your altar regularly is valuable, especially if you need a confidence boost before you head into a potential swoop situation.

Breathe in your altar's love. It's all about you.

You can even take a photo or a quick video of your altar. Having it on your device means you can give yourself a ROC boost anywhere and at any time.

Do yourself a favour and make your altar a part of your ROC ritual routine.

BE WRAPPED

You'll know when it's time to call on the ROC solid wrap.

This booster is especially nice to do after you have enjoyed a few minutes drinking in all the goodness of your altar.

And you do your ROC wrap in your mind, so it's available 24/7.

The idea of the wrap is to cloak yourself in the most positive protective energy you can find. Superman and Wonder Woman were both caped crusaders who used them when they needed to.

HOW TO GET YOUR ROC WRAP ON:

1. Notice when you need to wrap yourself. Maybe you feel a little fragile, or know confusion is coming.

2. Close your eyes and soften your eyelids.

3. Take a few soothing ROC breaths. Breathe in deeply through your nose and exhale gently through your mouth to calm your nervous system.

4. Imagine your wrap draped around your shoulders, moulding to your back, arms and chest.

5. Feel how safe you are.

6. Notice the incredible material your wrap is made from. It lets good flow in for you to enjoy, and out for others to enjoy. But it deflects all negative or anti-ROC thoughts and feelings.

7. Stand strong in your wrap. You are protected.

8. Wrap yourself often and let it boost you up so you can ROC and rise.

With Earth having so much free energy to share around, it makes sense to use it.

GET GROUNDED

Kick off your shoes and take a walk on nature's freebies—sand, grass, rocks, river beds and the like.

Why? Science tells us that Earth is a massive ball of flowing energy that's always moving and shifting. And we get to see it firsthand when volcanoes erupt and waves tug at the boards of surfers.

When your feet are free they absorb Earth's negative electrons, which your body thrives on to stay in balance. It's a handy way to find peace among chaos and reset yourself.

And with Earth having so much free energy to share around, it makes sense to use it when you:

» become distracted, emotional or a bit scatty

» start overthinking and losing sight of what's important to you

» feel anxious, edgy or highly reactive

» get dragged into drama

» feel totally out of sorts, and not really present

» need to balance yourself before entering a potential swoop situation

» need to restore calm in yourself after being in a swoop situation

HOW TO GET GROUNDED:

1. Take off your shoes.

2. Allow Earth's balancing electrons to naturally flow up through your feet and throughout your entire body by walking:

   » on grass (if it's wet, great!)   » on soil

   » in the mud (glorious mud)   » on sand

   » on raw concrete   » on tiles

   » on the beach   » on slate

   » in the ocean   » on rocks

3. Focus on what happens when your feet and Earth meet. Some would say it's a match made in heaven.

Barefoot walking lets Earth's natural substances move past insulating shoes.

Sand, grass, slate, rocks, mud, soil, beach, raw concrete and water are all waiting for you.

Kick off your shoes. Get grounded.

CONFIDENCE BOOSTERS

There will be times in your life when your confidence will take a hit. That's when you've got to be your own biggest fan, dig deep, believe and love yourself all the way to the moon and back.

Daily boosters will remind you of your worth and give you the edge you need to be your awesome self.

And when you boost yourself, you boost your crew too. So it's a win win.

CONFIDENCE BOOSTER: SIZE OF THE DOG

When I met my husband 20-odd years ago, he was wearing his favourite t-shirt—a cotton tee emblazoned with this quote from American writer Mark Twain: "It's not the size of the dog in the fight, it's the size of the fight in the dog." And keeping these wise words company were two dogs: one insanely strong, imposing and built like a truck, and the other much less so.

His t-shirt reminds me that sometimes life dishes out stuff that forces you to be courageous in the most profound ways. 'Courage' is such an incredible word, layered in strength and bravery. It comes from the Latin word *cor*, meaning 'heart'. I collect hearts (not human ones), and have done for many years. They remind me to have courage when I need it the most.

*Your point of difference
is your mental fitness
and your ability to
ROC and rise.*

Your heart is amazing. It's roughly the size of your fist at the moment, and will grow to twice that size by the time you're an adult. Sitting in your chest, it will beat about 2.5 billion times in your lifetime. And I'd bet my last dollar it will give you all the courage you need to face whatever life puts in your path.

My hubby's tee pointed out loud and clear that your point of difference isn't your height, your looks, your accent or your clothes. None of that matters when you need to push through a tough situation or dig deep when life throws you a curveball.

Your point of difference is your mental fitness and your ability to ROC and rise. And for that you don't need bulging biceps or a super toned butt, nor do you need to be loud, heroic and constantly in people's faces. ROC happens below the surface—no song and dance required.

With the help of your beating heart and your ever-growing ROC solid mindset, you can handle all the twists and turns in your life today, tomorrow, and the day after that. Yes, you can.

Love yourself.

CONFIDENCE BOOSTER: THE LOVE YOU LIST

Every time you love yourself, you're ramping up your ROC level and helping yourself stay above the line.

When was the last time you *loved* yourself and all your talents, quirks, skills and idiosyncrasies? Your LOVE YOU collection will lift you up and give you a boost whenever you need it.

Your **LOVE YOU LIST** covers everything that makes you … well, you. If you love something about yourself, write it down here and refer to it whenever you need a confidence boost.

_____

_____

_____

_____

_____

_____

_____

_____

CONFIDENCE BOOSTER: THE LEARNING TO LOVE YOU LIST

Let's not forget all the things you're *learning* to love about yourself. They need space too. Let this list grow on you and give it permission to boost rather than block you.

Your **LEARNING TO LOVE YOU** list covers *everything* that makes you you.

If there's something about yourself you're not totally in love with yet, but you're getting there, write it here:

_____

_____

_____

_____

_____

_____

_____

_____

_____

_____

*It feels good when
people notice your
unique shining traits.*

SHOW UP AND SHINE

To be ROC is to be real.

By now you've probably worked out that perfection exists in a land far away. How you walk, talk, dance and sing is totally up to you.

This is where I'd like to speak to the personality traits you proudly show your teachers, your family and your crew. These are the traits you allow to shine, probably because they're socially accepted or viewed as 'normal' (whatever that is).

It's your shine that lets you be yourself and own it.

A simple way to think about your shine is to focus on the aspects of you that get complimented on or acknowledged by your friends, family, coaches and teachers.

Like most people, you probably want your shine to be noticed. You don't have to do it loudly or even publicly. You can also do it quietly and behind the scenes. It feels good when people notice your unique shining traits and qualities as much as they do your hair, weight, height and latest test score.

Yes, it's nice to be noticed by others. But you're the expert on you, and so the most powerful way to show up and shine is to notice yourself. Claim your shine.

Now's a great time to get busy and brainstorm all the ways you shine.

Don't skip this section. Promise yourself that you'll do it.

This is such an important task. And you should do it as often as you can. Tag this page and flick back to it when you need to.

This is a gentle and boosting ritual that can knock some serious sense into you, especially when you've got the wobbles and aren't feeling as ROC solid as you could be.

I don't want to flood this page with examples. Instead I want you to trust your gut, follow your heart, and let all your shine light up the page. You might even like to copy your shine collection and add it to your altar or your V&V board.

Go on. Do it.

SHINE

Chill out in your hygge haven and write your shine traits on the opposite page.

Everyone has a flipside. But whether you choose to make friends with both sides is up to you.

WHERE THERE'S SHINE, THERE'S SHADE

Shine and shade, along with being above and below the line, are both a natural part of life. And you need both because they play such an important role in the ebb and flow of your life.

Now that you've shown up and noticed how you shine, it's time to flip the coin and look at the other side of yourself. It's no better or worse, just another part of the complete you.

Everyone has a flipside. But whether you choose to make friends with both sides is up to you.

To truly believe in yourself, build yourself up and back yourself, I suggest you shake hands with the parts of your personality (your so-called weaknesses) that sit quietly in the shade.

A friendly handshake with yourself will pave the way for you to totally love and respect your lighter, brighter side, without worrying whether others think you're 'too much', 'too loud', 'too confident' or 'not enough'.

When you accept your shine and your shade, you'll be more willing to step forward and say "Yes" to challenges that come with no guarantee.

But this isn't a quick fix you can do overnight. It takes time, work, patience, and a bucketload of courage and bravery.

You've got this.

SHADE and SHINE
NIGHT and DAY
UP and DOWN

Have you heard the saying 'finders keepers'? This idiom dates back to ancient Rome where the first person to find something unowned or abandoned could legally claim it as their own, and in doing so become the rightful owner.

By finding your shade first, you're claiming what's already yours. The shiny, the wacky and the shady.

As you get better at owning your shade, you'll find you're less affected by people pointing out your weaknesses or harping on about your shade shortfalls. That's because you found it first. You own it, and now you're working on it.

Your resilience will build, and other people's actions, words and choices will affect your ROC level less. They'll be like water running off a duck's back (providing they keep oiling their feathers).

Learning to make friends with your shade—without shame, embarrassment or unnecessary guilt blocking you and dulling your spark—is a lifelong process. But you have nothing to lose and everything to gain by starting now.

Of course, other people may try to bring you down. But you have absolutely no control over other people's choices or actions. You only have control over yourself—how you think, and how you respond or react to whatever comes your way.

Your so-called weakness
could be your most
profound teacher
in life.
You are enough.
You ROC.

As you get better at owning your shade, you'll find you're less affected by people pointing out your weaknesses.

CLAIM YOUR SHADE

Retreat to your *hygge* haven and write down your shady traits.

_____

_____

_____

_____

_____

_____

_____

_____

_____

_____

_____

_____

_____

MAKE PEACE WITH YOUR SHADE

You might be wondering how to move your shade to shine once you've found it and claimed it. It's one of the most commonly asked questions, so you're definitely among friends.

When I met Jasmine, she was wrestling with jealousy. It was one of her shady traits, and it was holding her back in her friendship group because she feared her best friend would be snatched away by other girls. Or new girls. Or any girls.

Jealousy is a normal human emotion. It's often referred to as 'the green-eyed monster', which was first coined by Shakespeare in *Othello* many moons ago.

While jealousy is a well-known term, I bet you don't shout it from the rooftop when you feel it rising up within you. Instead, like Jasmine, you sweep it under the rug because it's embarrassing when the green-eyed monster starts running the show.

It's good to keep in mind that just like anger, frustration, loneliness, fear, worry and doubt, jealousy is often temporary and comes and goes in waves.

If you treat it like a message being delivered by a postie you'll get curious, crack it wide open, and look inside to find out what it's all about.

Jealousy, and it's other below-the-line friends, can make your heart pound and your thoughts run wild. It can even cause knee-jerk reactions such as saying things you wouldn't normally say or acting in a way that's irrational and unkind.

To lessen the likelihood of sliding down this slippery slope, try following these steps.

STEP 1: NAME IT

What's the feeling that you're feeling? If it feels like jealousy then it is jealousy. Don't complicate it. Just give it a name that makes sense to you.

STEP 2: CLAIM IT

Say the name in your head or out loud, write it down, or tell someone you trust.

"I'm feeling jealous right now."

"Right now, I feel jealous."

STEP 3: OWN IT

Check in with your body talk to identify where that emotion has set up camp. Is it in your tummy, jaw or lower back, or has it hijacked your shoulders?

*Jealousy often shows
up to teach you
something big.*

If you've got a jealous feeling in your belly, breathe in deeply though your nose and imagine you're directing fresh and soothing oxygen to your belly. Sit with this. Just breathe and imagine.

You might even like to shake it off Harry style, which will also free any trapped emotions.

STEP 4: UNDERSTAND IT

Jealousy often shows up to teach you something big. It's powerful, and tries with all its might to protect any niggling little fears you may have from being found out.

If you're feeling fear but it's showing up as jealousy, it's time to ask yourself what you're scared of.

In Jasmine's case, she feared she would be left out, be forgotten, or lose her best friend.

Don't judge your shade as being right or wrong, or look for hidden meanings. Trust that you're ready to understand it so you can pull yourself back above the line where you belong.

Write down any fears that jump into your mind. Read the sentence starters and let your fears flow out of your mind and onto the page. (You can follow these steps for any shady parts of yourself that you'd like to shine instead.)

I fear:

_____

_____

I'm fearful that:

_____

_____

I'm afraid that:

_____

_____

I'm scared of:

_____

_____

Nice work. Now you have:

> » named your shade
> » claimed your shade
> » understood your shade

There's just one step to go. And this is the fun part that really helps you ROC and rise.

STEP 5: LIFT IT

Lifting is all about making peace with your shady thoughts and ideas.

Instead of fear, I choose to trust:

_____

_____

_____

Instead of fearful thoughts, I choose to believe:

_____

_____

_____

If I wasn't afraid, I would choose to think:

_____

_____

_____

I let go of scared thoughts and choose to accept:

_____

_____

_____

As a human you need social interaction to connect, learn and thrive. But you also need time with yourself.

TIME WITH YOURSELF

If you decide that being with yourself is the same as being lonely, you'll quickly turn to thoughts of lacking, exclusion, and fear of missing out. If that happens, you might rely on social media to fill the gap.

And that can be a very dangerous trap.

Like any new habit, building up your ability to spend time with yourself will call on your confidence, your belief that you'll be okay, and being okay when you hang out with yourself. It's a good thing, but if you're not used to it then give it time and practice. At first you may think something is missing, and that a gaping hole is begging to be filled.

That's okay. It will pass.

As a human you need social interaction to connect, learn and thrive. But you also need time with yourself—just you, amazing you—free from distractions and the influence of others. You don't have to be around other people to feel complete. You are enough.

Your thoughts can wander. They can even try to sabotage you by saying, "You're all alone, which means you're lonely, left out and forgotten."

Panic pops in for a visit, bringing anxious thinking along with it.

You may even start wondering what everyone else is doing right now, and whether you're missing out on something amazing.

Feel free to observe these thoughts. But don't give them too much of your precious energy. They're probably just showing up because you're trying something new. And that's okay. It's quite normal to react in a fearful way when things feel unfamiliar.

How you spend time with yourself is up to you. It might be sports, reading, watching Netflix, cooking, or getting creative. But whatever it is, do it often and make it part of your ROC and rise routine.

Making the decision to be alone will help you to appreciate yourself, your thoughts and your emotions on a whole new level. Over time you'll be more relaxed and comfortable in your own company, whether by your own choice or through circumstance. And it will get easier as your confidence builds.

Your thoughts have a huge part to play in making the most of your 'you' time. Above-the-line thoughts will see you rise above any fears and feelings of lacking. This will bring your attention back to the benefits of spending time with yourself, which some consider the ultimate sign of confidence.

Give it a try.

This powerful ROC habit starts with a single thought: to spend time with yourself.

Start small. Do it for five minutes, then ten, and then 15. Before you know it, you'll be feeling much more confident and making sure 'you time' is part of your personal ROC routine.

Remember to spend time
with the most important
person in your life—
YOU.

Confidence is an inside job that can't be handed over to somebody else.

The Confidence Recap – Section 4

You're storming ahead now.

This section has added even more tools to your ever-growing ROC and rise selection. I hope you now realise that confidence is an inside job that can't be handed over to somebody else. Here's a summary of the 11 user-friendly and super practical tools and confidence boosters you now need to practise.

1. **The Big Six Questions** – These are perfectly normal questions to ask. And it's okay if you don't have all the answers.

2. **Go to your altar** – That sacred place which feels like home and makes you smile.

3. **Be wrapped in your ROC wrap** – Which lets only good in and good out.

4. **Be grounded** – So your feet and body flow back in balance using Earth's energy.

5. **Size of the dog** – It's your courage that counts.

6. **Love you** – Go on, do it. Remind yourself that you love yourself and everything that makes you you.

7. **Learn to love you** – Accepting all of you, even the parts you've hidden in the past.

8. **Show up and shine** – You have talents and strengths. Enjoy them.

9. **Shine and shade** – No-one is perfect and able to shine all the time.

10. **Make peace with your shade** – Parts of your personality are begging for attention.

11. **Time with yourself** – You're the most important person in your life.

Notes & ROC Reminders

Take some time to reflect on what you've read in Section 4 about confidence. What caught your eye? What thoughts and ideas were triggered? What do you want to make sure you don't forget?

_____

_____

_____

_____

_____

_____

_____

_____

_____

_____

_____

_____

CONCLUSION

One day I got to have coffee with a well-known public speaker—someone I considered a guru in the space. As we talked, he was telling me all the non-negotiables for successful speaking.

One of the things he mentioned was that the very best speakers always have a perfectly manicured, highly detailed and finely tuned speech. (You know. The piece of paper they carefully unfold as they step up onto the stage and walk towards the lectern.)

As he spoke, my thoughts ran wild. My stomach launched into a squirming flip, my face reddened, and my heart started racing.

Why? Because when I speak to audiences I just stand and talk. My words flow from the knowledge in my mind and the memories in my heart.

I never have a perfectly manicured speech.

But the guru knew what he was talking about, right? After all, he was the expert.

So the next time I was booked to speak to a large high school, I decided to depart from my usual preparation method. Instead of creating my trusted framework of using guiding notes to support carefully selected pictures and quotes, I sat at my desk for hours and wrote a detailed, finely-tuned speech.

My son popped his head into my office and asked what I was doing. I told him I was writing a speech for my next speaking engagement. He looked at me strangely. "You don't usually do that."

I ignored his words and carried on.

Writing that speech was hard work for me. It didn't flow, it felt unnatural, and it took me ages to complete. But I did it anyway because that's what the professionals do. Apparently.

Fast forward to presentation day. I packed my laptop, laser pointer and spare batteries (just in case). I quickly grabbed the A4 paper folded on my desk, slid it into my laptop case next to my water bottle and headed to the car.

As I was driving I felt weird. My heart talk and body talk were out of sorts. Something wasn't right.

Fast forward to presentation time. Having been introduced to the audience, I stepped up the stairs and approached the lectern with my clicker and folded paper in hand. I was a little more nervous than usual, but I tried to focus on the story I was about to tell. (I always start with a story. It settles my heart and reminds me to be where my feet are. It works every time.)

After sharing my story and scanning the sea of faces in front of me, I opened the sheet of paper containing my speech and started pressing the creases out.

I looked down, ready to read the opening line of my perfectly manicured script ...

Only to see I didn't have my speech. I had an itemised garden centre receipt listing all the plants I'd bought for my garden the previous week.

My thoughts plummeted below the line to a place of total embarrassment and panic.

My heart skipped a beat, my legs turned to jelly, my stomach flipped and it felt as if every litre of blood was trying to escape from my body.

*My thoughts were
diving to a land of
defeat. What would
the guru say now?*

My face was pulsing red. Even my neck and ears were glowing.

Houston, we have a problem.

I took a breath and wondered what on earth I was going to do. Hundreds of eyes were staring at me, with their owners silently wondering, *Is this what 'professionals' do?*

My thoughts were diving to a land of defeat. What would the guru say now? How would he suggest I recover from such a disaster?

I knew I had to push my thoughts back up above the line. I brought my attention back to my feet by wriggling my toes in my shoes. I took a couple of ROC breaths: big, slow and deep. And then I paused, and reminded myself what I do best.

I looked up to the screen and read the title of my presentation.

Trusting YOU.

Oh, the irony!

But it also pointed out the way forward lay in reclaiming my thoughts, my trust in myself, my way and my style.

Holding the A4 garden centre receipt in my hands I said, "I want to tell you a real-life story about trusting, un-trusting, and thinking on your feet."

For the next hour I shared my story of meeting the guru and how, over a cup of coffee, I ended up following a below-the-line pathway that made me stop believing in myself.

Big mistake made, but an even bigger lesson learned.

Turning failure into opportunity, I trusted myself once again, went with the flow, and told hundreds of students a story about trusting and believing in themselves.

And that's where I hope this book has taken you. A place where you have tools and tactics to trust and believe in yourself when life's challenges take your thoughts and actions below the line.

NOW GO MAKE SOME NOISE!

Whenever I present to audiences filled with teenagers just like you, I arrive early so I can observe you as you filter in. There are usually a couple of hundred of you talking and laughing as you make your way into the theatre or large open space. You're all hustling and bustling for the best seat in the house—right next to your mate or bestie. There's a lot of noise, but the vibe is good. *Really* good.

When the time is right I get introduced to you all, and my presentation's title appears on the brightly lit screen. Then there's silence, as if someone has pressed the mute button. Quiet fills the entire space. It's the same quiet that shows up whenever there's a conversation about mental health and fitness. Strangely, it rarely happens when you talk about food, sport, parties, movies or holidays overseas. So I'm wondering:

> » Where has the noise gone?

> » Why are you all so silent?

> » Did I say something wrong?

I think to myself.

You're the generation to crack open the silence and get the conversation flowing.

You're the ones to make the change, be the change and lead the change.

You have the power to halt the hush and replace it with the most beautiful above-the-line noise, talk, laughter, questions and banter about mental fitness—yours, mine, theirs and ours.

You're the ones to make the change, be the change and lead the change in your own unique way, because your way is enough. Together with your crew and Dream Team, your collective effort will create the shift and build the momentum so everyone can ROC and rise.

It's time to bust the myths of far-fetched perfection portrayed on highly edited smiles that hide a thousand sighs.

It's time to speak face to face and eye to eye.

It's time to make a fresh start, hold your head high, and boost the thoughts in your mind.

You now have all the fundamentals, rituals, switch tools and boosters you need to do it. Interrupt the awkward hush and turn up the volume on ROC.

You're part of the ROC revolution.

You decide what goes up and what goes down. Your curious mind is ready for you to step up and be part of your mentally fit generation.

Be seen and be heard, because people all around the world are waiting for you to ROC and rise.

Now is the time.

Go gently my friend, but let nothing stand in your way.

Go make some noise!

ACKNOWLEDGEMENTS

From the bottom of my heart, I would like to thank:

Teenagers, thank you for being you and allowing me to be a part of your teenage journey, it's an honour. You show up with incredible courage and determination to find out what you're truly capable of.

The teenagers who read this book during its creation, I value your feedback, suggestions and the time you volunteered to our meet-ups. Our discussions were brilliant!

Parents and carers in the lives of teenagers, I have huge admiration for you and it's my privilege to help you equip your children with the skills and tools needed to handle life's ups and downs.

Event planners and educators, I am most grateful for your support of the prevention-focussed mental and emotional fitness messages I share at your events.

Kelly Exeter, from our first meeting you totally understood what I wanted to achieve. Your grace and wisdom meant my book was always safe in your hands.

Bill Harper and Kym Campradt, I appreciate your flawless attention to detail.

Social media supporters, I value your loyalty, likes and shares. They all help to spread ROC messages so teenagers can keep driving their resilience, optimism and confidence UP.

Nicky Tillyer, my 'creative friend' who helped give energy to the term 'ROC', I wish we lived closer!

Des Smith, my unofficial mentor as I established my career. You left this earth way too soon, but I often ask, "What would Des think?"

My grandparents who were my forever teachers and secret keepers. You believed in me. Always.

My mum, Heather, you are the best listener and giver of time. Your support during the writing of this book has been amazing and I can't thank you enough for being the awesome grandmother you are to your grandson Caiden.

My husband Justin, son Caiden and our dog Harry. Our little family has always been so full of unconditional love and respect, I couldn't be a more content wife and proud mum. I love you to the moon and back.

ABOUT THE AUTHOR

Claire Eaton is a parent, youth coach, ROC Mindset speaker and author who lives in Perth, Western Australia.

One of Australia's freshest advocates for youth and prevention-based mental fitness, Claire's dream is for all teenagers to have access to ROC boosting tools and skills. With more resilience, optimism and confidence, teenagers will be better equipped to take charge of their own mental fitness as they play the game we call life.

Claire draws on experience gained from more than two decades as an educator, deputy principal, university tutor, youth mentor and performance coach. She's been speaking about ROC and coaching teenagers and their families in private practice since 2008. She combines her long-held passion for mental health and knowledge of youth development to help young people and their families boost their mental and emotional fortitude—something that's desperately needed in today's fast-paced world.

When Claire isn't working with teenagers or speaking to audiences around Australia, she's happily living a simple and contented life with her hubby, her son and their dog.

ROC and Rise is her first book.

You can find out more at
ClaireEaton.com.au

Notes & ROC Reminders

Take some time to reflect on what you've read in this book. What thoughts and ideas were triggered? What do you want to make sure you don't forget? What actions will you take?

_____

_____

_____

_____

_____

_____

_____

_____

_____

_____

_____

_____

_____

9 780648 537007